D0104017

TO SPREAD THE
POWER

TO SPREAD THE
POWER

Church Growth in the Wesleyan Spirit

GEORGE G. HUNTER III

Abingdon Press
Nashville

To Spread the Power

Library of Congress Cataloging-in-Publication Data

HUNTER, GEORGE G.
  To spread the power.
  Bibliography: p. 213
  Includes index.
  1. Church growth. 2. Wesley, John, 1703-1791.
  I. Title.
  BV652.25.H84   1987   254'.5   86-26507

ISBN 0-687-42259-0 (alk. paper)

Manufactured by the Parthenon Press at
Nashville, Tennessee, United States of America

I dedicate this book to four lifelong friends

John Ed Mathison
Fraser Memorial United Methodist Church
Montgomery, Alabama

Ed Beck
Sunrise United Methodist Church
Colorado Springs, Colorado

Brad Dinsmore
Lake Magdalen United Methodist Church
Tampa, Florida

Harold Bales
First United Methodist Church
Charlotte, North Carolina

without whom this book was written,
but who, nevertheless, practice what I preach!

FOREWORD

Church Growth and John Wesley—what a combination! And who better to do it than George "Chuck" Hunter.

At a time when we desperately need both diagnosis and design in evangelism, Dr. Hunter probes and recommends with clarity and intensity. *To Spread the Power: Church Growth in the Wesleyan Spirit* helps every reader, every Christian, better understand the dynamics of making disciples.

The book is a bridge between a biblical-Wesleyan foundation on one hand and Church Growth-social science moorings on the other. Few writers have as complete a grasp of the tested principles of Church Growth. Few writers understand the Wesleyan revival as well as Hunter does. Few people could draw so deeply on both traditions to help us in our evangelistic work today.

And help we need. With the twenty-five-year decline of Protestantism's mainline churches, thoughtful, prayerful church leaders are searching for guidance. We are recovering from a long period of amnesia. When I wrote *And Are We Yet Alive?*, I hoped others would go deeper, go farther. Chuck Hunter has done that.

To Spread the Power moves us forward. Look at some of his observations:

• Much of the Church Growth movement is consistent with Wesleyan principles. Wesley sensed "spiritually" some truths that can now be authenticated "scientifically."

• The class meeting is reproducible today, dressed up in modern clothing. Growing churches today study Acts 2 and the Wesleyan class meeting.

• Certain disciple-making principles we thought applied only to overseas missions actually apply to mission field U.S.A. We can see more clearly at a distance. We can learn from our spiritual children.

• Church revitalization, congregational growth, and making disciples is neither magic nor mystery. Many tested guidelines have consistently shown themselves to contain the power of God—in New Testament times, in the great Wesleyan revival, and in growing churches today.

In reading the manuscript, I was inspired by the constant swing between theory and practice. Here is a valid principle, writes Hunter; here is how it works in Tampa, Florida, or Wilmington, Delaware. I was also enthused, as you will be, to observe how McGavran and Wesley targeted "responsive" people, how they both used indigenous music and language and culture, how they identified needs and met them, and how determined both were to have supportive fellowship groups, lest converts die "aborning."

Experts will read this book; so will beginners. People struggling to help their churches grow will be instructed and inspired. Students of the Bible and of growth principles will experience a synthesis of ideas, putting separate ideas into a wholistic concept of evangelism.

I'm glad the book is named *To Spread the Power*. All growth in the church comes from the power of the Holy Spirit. John Wesley understood that. But human instrumentality can be helpful or harmful, appropriate or inappropriate in spreading the power. Wesley understood that too.

The delight of George Hunter's book is that it will help you understand more clearly the power of God and the work and witness of the faithful. I heartily recommend it to every Christian believer.

Richard B. Wilke

C O N T E N T S

When first sent forth to minister the word,
Say, did we preach ourselves, or Christ the Lord?
Was it our aim disciples to collect,
To raise a party, or to found a sect?
No; but to spread the power of Jesu's name,
Repair the walls of our Jerusalem
Revive the piety of ancient days,
And fill the earth with our Redeemer's praise.

—Charles Wesley, 1744

INTRODUCTORY

Why *another* Church Growth book? By now the Church Growth market is glutted with more books than Christian leaders can read, and many consumers have been "burned" by purchasing rehash. The market is still hot, but any new book ought to justify its existence.

Several features may recommend this book to the wary. First, after fifty years of Church Growth research, reflecting, and refining, we can now systematize much of the essential content, and bring people on board more quickly. Second, after a fallow half decade, there are now new research conclusions, insights, and case studies worth adding to the lore of Christian evangelism. Third, this book reaches back to draw from John Wesley as a major strategic mind, in addition to twentieth-century leaders, thereby providing the growing Church Growth literature with some needed historical, theological, and strategic depth.

The mission of this book is to teach local Christian leaders, lay and clergy, how to evangelize, that is, how to communicate the gospel, make new disciples, and lead local Christian movements effectively. The book emphasizes six perennial "mega-strategies" of evangelism that will be useful into the next century, universal principles that can be adapted to any mission situation, any time, any place. The reader will never have to unlearn the six principles presented in this book. At the same time, thorough knowledge of the six principles will enable the evangelistic leader to more readily assimilate and use new approaches and methods as they emerge.

The book's mission involves liberating Christians from three entrenched myths that have long frustrated the effectiveness of evangelism.

One is the myth that one takes a "magic" approach to reaching people. Many Christians assume, like our primitive pre-Christian ancestors, that supernatural victories are achieved through "incantations," that learning, saying, and doing the right things right will trigger victory in the spiritual realm. By such a pre-Christian script, Christians try one "magical formula" after another. Or, they vow to do nothing at all until denominational headquarters produces the perfect stretch sock to fit every situation! In fact, no magic exists in these matters, in part because methods do not evangelize. Rather, faithful compassionate *people* evangelize, empowered by the Spirit, using whatever methods or words are most natural or useful in a situation.

If the first myth takes refuge in "magic," the second takes refuge in "mystery." Many Christians assume that whatever is involved in making new disciples is so complex, deep, and mysterious that it is futile to try. This myth is invalid because God frequently builds on our fragmentary understanding and multiplies our few loaves and fishes. It is also untrue because Church Growth now offers proven knowledge to dispel the immobilizing mystery. Church Growth does *not* offer a new "research-proven magic" or any one method that will reach all people. It does offer principles and infinitely adaptable strategies and the knowledge that frees Christians to discover or devise the methods, which in a given setting with a given people, will help cultivate and gather the harvest.

The third myth from which Christians need liberating is "modernity." This myth reflects the obsessional fascination with what is "new," "trendy," or even "on the horizon" in evangelism (and everything else), an affliction especially epidemic among mainline Protestants. However, Church Growth people focus on what is "true," whether or not it is "new." The major principles behind Christianity's expansion are *perennial*, and while the principles require adaptation to each particular culture and situation, potential evangelizers are stronger for mastering the perennial principles than by stampeding toward "anything new."

The book makes use of insights and research methods from the behavioral and social sciences. Karl Barth was once asked, "What do you think of the behavioral sciences?" Barth replied, "I try not to." Since most of Christianity's objectives for people are achieved in regard to *personalities* who live in *societies,* such comfortable isolation from the behavioral and social sciences is a luxury that the Christian mission can no longer justify.

In using John Wesley as a primary source for Church Growth insight, I may have rushed in where more prudent eclectic minds would fear to tread. This is not a "Wesley book" *per se,* but a book using Wesley as one source among others. A paper by British Methodism's Geoffrey Harris first alerted me to investigate Wesley as a Church Growth source. I first attempted to delineate Wesley's significance in this area to a working group at the 1982 Oxford Institute on Methodist Theology. I do not write as an established Wesley scholar. I have not crossed the particular academic hurdles that qualify one to be a card-carrying member of that splendid club. My own graduate and post-graduate studies have focused, after two degrees in theology, on communication studies and applied behavioral sciences. In preparing this book I have read from Wesley's own voluminous writings, particularly his journal, letters, and certain essays. I am not immersed in the two hundred years of writing *about* Wesley, so I leave it to a more specialized mind to produce a more comprehensive and definitive study of Wesley as movement strategist and leader.

But I am not embarrassed by the gold that my background has permitted me to see in Wesley's writings. Indeed, I have been astonished at the amount of strategic wisdom that Wesley's successors and interpreters have passed over. I took the precaution of running drafts of two of the more vulnerable chapters past some real Wesley experts, and I thank Kenneth Kinghorn, Steve Harper, Robert Tuttle, and David Watson for their suggestions. I join Methodism in paying tribute to such senior scholars as William R. Cannon, Frank Baker, and Albert Outler, and to Asbury Theological

Seminary, for rescuing Wesley from the eclipse imposed by the previous generation, and for stimulating today's renaissance in Wesley studies. If this book should help some people called Methodists to recover from their long night of amnesia, I would be grateful.

I should also thank three other scholars—Darrell Whiteman (cultural anthropology), Philip Spottswood (psychology), and George Morris (evangelization), for their suggestions for strengthening certain chapters. I thank the many churches from which I gathered data and case studies; my accounts of such material usually represent the case at the time I gathered it. I thank my family, Ella Fay, Gill, Monica, Donny, and my mother, Barbara, for understanding my need to spend priority time with my personal computer. For extensive stimulation and suggestions, and for their tolerance of administrative tasks deferred, I thank my faculty and student colleagues in the new E. Stanley Jones School of World Mission and Evangelism of Asbury Theological Seminary in Wilmore, Kentucky.

Specifically, this is a second generation text on Church Growth strategies. I am aware that strategies alone do not a movement make, and that some variables in Christian mission are more important than strategy. Ultimately, the work of evangelistic mission is only done by Christians and Churches who: (a) see their identity in continuity with the apostles, (b) see the mission fields in which their churches are placed, (c) are open to the empowerment of the Spirit, and (d) desire above all else to join the Lord of the Harvest in finding the lost and in building that church against which the gates of hell and powers of death will not prevail.

I was reminded recently of how most of today's church is, tragically, preoccupied with lesser matters. Father Vincent J. Donovan, in *Christianity Rediscovered*, reports his experience of nineteen years as a missionary to the Masai tribes of eastern Africa. When he arrived, he observed that the established mission station had thriving schools, hospitals, and other institutions and services for the Masai, and that the relations between the missionaries and the Masai were excellent. Nevertheless, no Masai had become Christians, no indigenous

Masai church was being established, and Donovan's colleagues seemed so absorbed in the routine work of church and institutional life that they had forgot the apostolic dream that first lured them to Africa. Fearing that such absorption was occurring within himself, Donovan wrote a decisive letter to his bishop:

Masai kraals are visited very often . . . But never, or almost never, is religion mentioned on any of these visits . . . The relationship with the Masai, in my opinion, is dismal, time consuming, wearying, expensive, and materialistic . . . In other words, the relationship with the Masai, except the school children, goes into every area except that very one area which is most dear to the heart of the missionary . . . It looks as if such a situation will go on forever.

I suddenly feel the urgent need to . . . simply go to these people and do the work among them for which I came to Africa.

I would propose cutting myself off from the school and the hospital, as far as these people are concerned—as well as the socializing with them—and just go and talk to them about God and the Christian message . . .

That is precisely what I would propose to do. I know what most people say. It is impossible to preach the gospel directly to the Masai. They are the hardest of all the pagans, the toughest of the tough. In all their hundreds of years of existence, they have never accepted anything from the outside . . .

But I would like to try. I want to go to the Masai on daily safaris—unencumbered with the burden of selling them our school system, or begging for their children for our schools, or carrying their sick, or giving them medicine.

Outside of this, *I have no theory, no plan, no strategy, no gimmicks*—no idea of what will come. I feel rather naked. *I will begin as soon as possible.* (Donovan, 1978, pp. 14-16, emphasis added)

When Donovan explained to the first Masai chief what he proposed to do and why it was so important, the chief asked, understandably, "If that is why you came here, why did you wait so long to tell us about this?"

The institutional inertia Donovan found in the routine of his East Africa mission station has afflicted countless churches and church institutions on every continent, though what constitutes "mere church work" varies from one culture to another. For instance, a stereotypical American parish church may be absorbed in a routine of potluck suppers, bowling leagues, rummage sales, endless meetings, and a

hundred other programs and activities, and is at least as
unmindful of the Great Commission as any Third World
mission station.

Indeed, this problem afflicts even more a church, like most
of those in North America, in the "fourth stage" of Christian
mission. That is, when a denomination in a society is clearly
past (1) the early exploratory period, (2) the establishment of
mission stations and their ministries, and (3) the development
of an indigenous church, it is now strategically ready for (4)
the continuing challenge of wider evangelism within its
society (*see* McGavran, 1979, pp. 225ff.). There is, however,
something tragically seductive about a denomination reaching a stage of this continuing outreach where the pins on a
map show an established church in virtually every town in a
state or society; the denomination begins to think of outreach
as "finished" and settle in for the nurture and care of
Christians. These churches then experience net membership
decline until they rediscover their perennial apostolic
mission. This book's mission is to inform continuing
Christian evangelization at that fourth stage.

The most pressing need is for countless Christian
communities to remember their apostolic calling and "begin
as soon as possible." Those who do will discover, as did Father
Donovan, that the Church Growth tradition provides an
impressive body of theories, plans, and strategies—but no
"gimmicks."

The Recovery of
Apostolic Confidence

One morning in 1881 the Reverend C. C. McCabe sat on a train heading toward the Pacific Northwest of the United States. In a few days he would be leading the planning, later the fund raising, for planting Methodist churches over much of Oregon, Idaho, and Washington. Years before, he had been an influential chaplain in the Civil War. Now he was leader of new church extension for the Methodist Episcopal Church. A century before, the Methodists and Baptists had rivaled each other in planting churches across the spreading frontier. Methodism's early leader Francis Asbury had said of the Baptists: "Like ghosts they haunt us from place to place!" But now McCabe was trumpet, strategist, and fund-raiser for an achievement outpacing the Baptists. The Methodist Church was starting more than one new congregation a day. Some months they averaged *two* new churches a day. And now, Methodism was to be God's avant-garde in the Pacific Northwest.

An article in McCabe's morning newspaper featured a speech delivered in Chicago by Robert G. Ingersol, the famous agnostic philosopher, to a convention of the Freethinkers Association of America. Ingersol's speech declared that "the churches are dying out all over the earth; they are struck with death" (*see* Luccock, 1964, pp. 66-67). When the train stopped at the next town, McCabe sent a telegram to Ingersol, still at the convention:

Dear Robert:
"All hail the power of Jesus' name"—we are building one Methodist Church for every day in the year, and propose to make it two a day!

C. C. McCabe

Word about the telegram was leaked, and someone wrote a folk hymn that was sung throughout the Pacific Northwest in preaching missions and camp meetings, brush arbors and Sunday evening services. The song dramatized the frontier Methodist people's quiet confidence in the power of what they offered people:

> The infidels, a motley band,
>   In counsel met, and said:
> "The churches are dying across the land,
>   and soon they'll all be dead."
> When suddenly, a message came
>   And caught them with dismay:
> "All hail the power of Jesus' name,
>   We're building two a day!"
>
> We're building two a day, Dear Bob,
>   We're building two a day!
> All hail the power of Jesus' name,
>   We're building two a day.

C. C. McCabe was a model of apostolic confidence. The same apostolic confidence that drove McCabe has driven the leaders of every generation in which Methodism has moved forward, and I imagine this is the case with other Christian traditions too. Such apostolic confidence is originally mirrored in the Acts of the Apostles, which reflects the early movement's confidence in Whose they were, who they had become, and in the contagious power of what they offered humanity. In part, their apostolic confidence sprang from the life of Christ within them, and the power of his Spirit among them, and their resolve to live, or die, for the gospel. But, in part, their apostolic confidence welled within them as a by-product of apostolic competence. McCabe and other Methodists, too, were confident because they were compe-

20

tent, that is, their objectives were clear and they knew how to join the Spirit to achieve them.

Today's church is experiencing a rebirth of apostolic confidence. This confidence is emerging from two sources: the "Spiritual Formation" movement, pioneering in the depth of Christian inner life and power, and the "Church Growth" movement, whose research enables Christians to see communities through apostolic lenses and to understand how people are reached and how the faith spreads. Church Growth, however, is no mere technology that leaves the praying to others. In the words of Donald McGavran, the Church Growth movement's founder, it involves the discovery that, "It is God's will that His Church grow, that His lost children are found." Church Growth is a way of obeying God's will and loving him with our minds as well as our hearts. It is also academic, an applied behavioral science. For the (very occasional) reader who cannot rest without an academic definition, Church Growth is

an application of biblical, theological, anthropological, and sociological principles to congregations and denominations and to their communities in an effort to disciple the greatest number of people for Jesus Christ. Believing that "it is God's will that His Church grow, that His lost children are found," Church Growth endeavors to devise strategies, develop objectives, and apply proven principles of growth to individual congregations, to denominations, and to the worldwide Body of Christ.

Because of the Church Growth movement's discoveries, much of the Christian Church is, after decades of stagnation, a more confident and contagious movement in many mission fields across the earth. Leaders who once treaded water now walk on water!

Donald McGavran's Life Quest

Donald McGavran was, fifty years after McCabe's letter to Ingersol, the superintendent of Christian Church (Disciples of Christ) work in Central India. One year he studied the annual membership reports of 145 congregations. Of these,

134 churches were stagnant or declining, but 11 were growing 20 percent a year or more. He wondered why some churches grow and some do not. He began visiting churches, asking leaders "Why is your church growing?" or "Why isn't your church growing?" To his astonishment, they could not tell him! They thought of something to say—a hunch, excuse, bias, or rationalization—but nothing that a Columbia University Ph.D., schooled in the behavioral and social sciences, could have confidence in. Their responses were devoid of reasons and demonstrable causes for the church's growth or nongrowth. Sometimes their answers were contradictory. Leaders of a growing church would say, "We grow because we preach the pure Word of God," while leaders of declining churches would say, "We aren't growing because we preach the pure Word of God!"

McGavran saw that this matter needed objective research if defensible and useful answers were to be found. He began studying churches, becoming increasingly obsessed by three questions: (1) When a church is growing, *why* is it growing? What are the causes of church growth? (2) When a church is not growing, *why* isn't it growing? What are the barriers, obstructions, or sicknesses that prevent the natural life, vitality, and growth of churches? (3) His quest was not essentially academic, to satisfy curiosity or fill the stacks of libraries with additional arid tomes; so his big question was, What are the reproducible principles behind growing churches, principles that might be applied or adapted by churches with opportunity but not yet gathering the harvest? He was "observing what procedures God was blessing to the growth of his churches and what he was not" (McGavran and Hunter, 1980, p. 17).

McGavran engaged in this research, as anyone would, with some biases. He believed (1) the mandate of the church's mission is contained in our Lord's Great Commission (especially Matt. 28:19-20) and dramatized in the Acts of the Apostles. Consequently, he believed (2) the objective in evangelism is to make disciples, not merely to love people, or proclaim the gospel, or record "decisions" for Christ. He believed (3) two objectives for people are involved in making new disciples: that they become (a) followers of Christ and

(b) be incorporated into the body of Christ; and that these discrete objectives occur in either order. And he believed (4) the ministry of evangelism does not stop until new believers are active members of the church, involved with "the apostles' teaching and fellowship, to the breaking of bread and the prayers" (Acts 2:42), and that (5) you can tell when that kind of evangelism is taking place: The church is growing with integrity and power. To discern the reproducible causes behind the growth of such churches is the quest of Church Growth scholars. And those biases inform McGavran's definition of the ministry of evangelism as "Proclaiming Jesus Christ as God and Savior and persuading men and women to become His disciples and responsible members of His Church."

Actually, McGavran was slightly preceded in this research approach by a Methodist missionary in India, J. Wascom Pickett, whose *Christian Mass Movements in India* demonstrated that field research could show the way forward. Pickett and McGavran studied several churches together, and McGavran "lit my candle at Pickett's fire," mastered his research methods, added his own, and took up where Pickett left off. While Pickett spent the rest of his career in administration as a Methodist bishop, McGavran adhered to the Church Growth agenda for the next half century.

In research methods, Pickett mainly employed questionnaires and interviews. McGavran made less use of *questionnaires,* but greater use of *interviews,* to which he added the use of *observation* and *historical analysis.* Those four methods, though refined, remain the major methods of Church Growth research and much other mission-related research. Using graphs of church membership data as a visual tool, McGavran devised a streamlined approach to the otherwise awesome task of researching the history of a congregation or denomination. In McGavran's approach, one notes the sharp rises and declines in "the graph of growth." Then one does focused research in church minutes, publications, and so forth, and one interviews the people who were around at the time, to determine the probable causes of the graph's significant rises and falls. "What was happening when this took place?" "What could have caused this?" (*see* McGavran, 1980, chs. 6 and 7).

As McGavran could gain study leaves and research grants, he spent the next quarter century analyzing growing and nongrowing churches among caste peoples and tribal peoples of India, in several countries of western Africa, in Puerto Rico, the Philippines, Jamaica, Mexico, Japan, Zaire, and elsewhere. After establishing the Institute of Church Growth, and then Fuller Theological Seminary's School of World Mission, he directed the research of many other scholars. Today several hundred case studies have been published, including such exotic titles as *Animistic Aymaras and Church Growth, People Movements in the Punjab, Crucial Issues in Bangledesh, Church Growth in Southern Nigeria, Solomon Islands Christianity,* and *Church Growth in West New Guinea.* McGavran's own systematic conclusions were published in *The Bridges of God* (1955), *How Churches Grow* (1959), and *Understanding Church Growth* (1970, rev. ed. 1980). By this time McGavran had high-powered company in the research quest, notably Alan Tippett, Ralph Winter, and Peter Wagner. And they built upon the work of others, such as Roland Allen's early twentieth-century theories, Kenneth Scott Latourette's 7-volume *History of the Expansion of Christianity,* and the work by Eugene Nida in missionary anthropology.

In the 1970s, with the discovery that North America, too, is a mission field—with at least 155 million undiscipled pagans—leaders as diverse as Win Arn, Wendell Belew, Wagner, Paul Benjamin, Lyle Schaller, Charles Chaney, Ron Lewis, Eddie Gibbs, and this writer began championing Church Growth possibilities for churches in North America and Europe. Win Arn's films, such as "How to Grow a Church" and "The Great Commission Sunday School," popularized Church Growth ideas. Church Growth courses have entered the curricula of theological seminaries and church colleges. Church Growth thought has influenced much of the world church, especially since the 1974 Congress on Evangelization in Lausanne, Switzerland. Its insights increasingly script what many mission agencies and societies are doing and planning. The new or increased growth of many denominations in many nations reflects the diffusion of strategic ideas from Church Growth pens. Though the

Church Growth movement is *not* the "Mighty River" that one writer suggests, its growing influence is undeniable, particularly in the new lenses it grinds for church leaders to see their opportunity. Its influence is so considerable that some supporters assume it to be "a new thing under the sun"!

Church Growth's Mixed Company

Actually, the Church Growth approach is not unique. Its similarity to other approaches to organization effectiveness is reflected, for instance, in the Peters and Waterman phenomenon, *In Search of Excellence*. In the very early 1980s, many American businesses were running scared, having swallowed then prevailing myths about the omnicompetence of Japanese managers and organizations. But Tom Peters and Bob Waterman, two budding management gurus out of Stanford University and McKinsey & Company, saw that some American companies, in various fields, were very effective and achieved their objectives in good times and bad. They studied 61 "excellent companies," such as IBM, Xerox, Eastman Kodak, Proctor & Gamble, Exxon, Delta Airlines, and McDonald's, 21 in some depth. They (1) studied the recent *histories* of the companies, (2) interpreted *questionnaire* data from thousands of employees at every level, (3) *observed* the companies on site and recorded their impressions, and (4) conducted structured *interviews* with hundreds of key persons. Neither their four methods nor the package were original; people in "Organization Development" had employed the package for years. But their research purpose represented a distinct direction: They intended "to generalize about what the excellent companies seem to be doing that the rest are not" (Peters and Waterman, 1982, p. xxv). They sifted their mountains of data for two years until, gradually, eight principles shined forth like precious gems, polished with memorable language like "a bias for action," "close to the customer," "productivity through people," "value driven," "stick to the knitting," and "simple form, lean staff."

In Search of Excellence became the largest selling book on management in history. By 1985 it had sold more than 5 million copies in English and fifteen translations. The book's success illustrates that nothing is quite so powerful as an idea whose time has come. Many organizations and institutions are preoccupied with questions about "competency," "achievement," "effectiveness," "peak performance," and "excellence."

Church Growth shares much with the world's new interest in the effectiveness of organizations. Church Growth people have known for some time that what counts in Christian mission is not the church's mere "presence" or "concern," but whether hungry people are fed, estranged people are reconciled, injustice is rectified, and lost people are found. Probably no question in mission is more important than the effectiveness of what we do in Christ's name. Furthermore, Church Growth's research methods—historical analysis, observation, questionnaires, and interviews—are the same cluster of qualitative behavioral science research methods proven useful in companies, educational institutions, and other organizations. And, like Peters and Waterman, Church Growth people want to find out what effective growing churches are doing that the rest are not!

Whereas Church Growth shares Peters' and Waterman's concern for the effectiveness of an organization's mission, Church Growth's focus on the Christian faith's expansion overlaps wide concern in the behavioral sciences for knowing why and how various ideas, causes, and technologies spread in a society. This "research tradition" began in 1943, when rural sociologists at Iowa State University wanted to know why and how a new superior hybrid corn seed had rapidly and effectively "diffused" (spread) among corn farmers in one region of Iowa, but not another. They believed that if they knew *how* important innovations spread effectively, informed "change agents" could facilitate the process. Today, more than three thousand research studies in the diffusion of innovations have been published by scholars in rural sociology, communication, education, marketing, general sociology, public health and medical sociology, anthropology, and geography (*see* Rogers, 1983). Many of their conclusions, like many from organization effectiveness, have significant implications for the church's growth and greater effectiveness.

McGavran has a much earlier cousin in Aristotle, who wanted to know how, through effective public communication, people become convinced of truth and align themselves with noble causes. Aristotle studied transcripts of effective speeches of the past, observed effective and ineffective speakers and different kinds of audiences, and (presumably) interviewed speakers who were effective in legislative, judicial, and ceremonial settings. He devised a lecture course on the principles of effective discourse (or rhetoric) for his academy in Athens. His extensive notes were published posthumously as *The Rhetoric of Aristotle*. He wanted to know why a few speakers were so much more effective than others, in order to teach other advocates of truth and justice to communicate more effectively. He employed some of the methods McGavran was to use more than two thousand years later.

Aristotle concluded that it was more important for the strategic communicator to learn to analyze the audience and then adapt the form (but not the substance) of a speech to that audience. McGavran also emphasized audience analysis in his studied approach to communicating and spreading Christianity. Furthermore, Aristotle and McGavran share a similar promise for those who would learn from them: Aristotle did not promise that, with his principles well in mind, a lawyer's client would always be acquitted or a legislator's bill always passed; he claimed to impart the informed "faculty of discovering all the available means of persuasion in any given situation." Likewise, McGavran does not claim that anyone who studies Church Growth will reach every person or necessarily experience great church growth; he claims to develop leaders who can discover, in their given situation, the available means for reaching people and experiencing growth. And Church Growth, on the larger scale, helps leaders of judicatories and denominations to identify the opportunities for expanding their movement.

Another of McGavran's cousins, in more direct lineage, is Charles Grandison Finney, evangelist and leader of America's Second Great Awakening in the early decades of the nineteenth century. Finney's lucid insights were remarkable, and he found himself parting company with the mind of Jonathan Edwards (and the reigning assumption of the First

27

Great Awakening), who maintained that a general awakening or religious movement is a sovereign "miracle" of God that Christians have no significant role in bringing about. Though Christians may pray for a revival, any human role is passive. An awakening is a Sovereign act, and a surprise.

Finney did not discount the role of prayer in revival, or the action of God in bringing it about. But, in the first chapter of his celebrated *Lectures on Revivals of Religion,* Finney contends that an awakening or a revival is "not a miracle," if, by a miracle, one refers to God acting in a way that suspends the usual "laws" of the human mind and the human audience. Rather, God works *through* those laws of human mind and audience to achieve his purposes, and the more Christians understand those laws, or principles, the greater role Christians can play in working with God to create a movement toward faith. Finney saw how much God has entrusted to the church's mission, and how the church is called to think and strategize, as well as pray, about effectively achieving evangelistic objectives. Donald McGavran would concur with Finney's stance on employing, say, psychology and crowd psychology, but would add (and depend more on) the insights of sociology and anthropology. Church Growth "draws heavily on the social sciences because it always occurs in societies" (McGavran, 1980, p. vii).

Donald McGavran's orientation and driving ideas are also remarkably like those of John Wesley. Mr. Wesley knew what he was doing in leading the expansion of eighteenth-century British Methodism. Much of what he knew came from reflection on data that he collected. He discovered, and taught, several of the major strategic themes that modern Church Growth has (re)discovered. Indeed, the mind of Wesley is such an important ("missing") link in the history of Church Growth thought that we devote the next chapter to exploring it.

On the Validity of the Church Growth Approach

Why do we believe in and advocate the Church Growth approach? In the ministry of evangelism, it would not occur to many Christians to do research to inform what we do in evangelism! Demonstrating McGavran's consistency with folks from Aristotle to Wesley and Finney, to Peters and Waterman, may be interesting, and may help Church Growth to appear more plausible and less maverick. But why jump aboard this bandwagon?

I believe this is best answered by wrestling with a more foundational question: Why do any of us do what we do in the ministry of evangelism? One chap passes out tracts, another stands on a soap box to address an open air crowd, another visits door to door, another leads a lunchtime Bible study for colleagues, another invites people to church, and still another takes his church into people's homes through television. Why does each person do, specifically, what he or she does in the name of "evangelism"? I have been curious about this for several years. I have observed and interviewed many practicing evangelicals, asking, "Where did you get that?" "Why did you start doing it that way?" There are many sources and models for evangelistic activity.

For instance, sometimes the source is *subjective*. In this category, people report they do it "that way" because "that is the method that reached me." Others report that it is what they "enjoy," or "like," or "turns me on." Still others report that their method "seems right to me." One couple stated, "We just feel good and close to God when we do this." One woman always gives her testimony because "it always helps me and strengthens my faith."

However, other people's source for what they do in evangelism is some *norm in* their reference group or Christian subculture. People have reported, "That is the way we have always done it," or "Our Presbytery has a program this year, and we have a manual and filmstrip showing how we'll all be doing it," or "It's the Lutheran way," or "That is the way we learned in seminary." Christians of certain liturgical traditions employ, in prescribed ways, the holy days and seasons, the rites of passage, and even pilgrimages in seeking their evangelistic objectives.

Still other people use some *external authoritative* source for their evangelism method. Some are following the direct leading of the Holy Spirit. Others are using Paul's performance at Mars Hill as their model, or Jesus' conversation with the woman at the well, or a particular book of the Bible—or selections from it—such as the Roman Road. Others copy a model evangelist. Others place confidence in the way a particular successful church does it. A very few follow some theologian's prescription! A fair number follow the formula of a para-church organization, such as the "Four Spiritual Laws" of Campus Crusade. Others follow the model of an authoritative group, such as the Latin American Poor or some Roman Catholic order. Others are driven by a moral imperative, concluding that love (or gratitude, or duty) leaves us no choice, and their understanding of the imperative shapes what they do. Still others follow or utter a formula that is, like magic, believed to bring about the desired results.

Others "do their thing" from some _logical,_ or _common sense, source_. Some approaches use a deduction from a truth claim within a doctrinal system, such as a behavioral definition of the elect. Other approaches use an induction from some specific insight, perhaps an insight about human nature. Others operate using a maxim from folk wisdom, such as "Honey attracts more flies than vinegar." Still others experiment until they find an approach that seems to fit them and seems to work. Others are more rigorously pragmatic, using whatever is supposed to work. Some Christians interview a person long enough to discern where he or she is hurting, and then offer the facet of the gospel that is great news for that need.

Some Christians use _secular_ sources for what they do in a ministry of evangelism. For instance, one fellow said "I sell religion the same way I sell appliances—salesmanship!" Others engage in the "behavior-specific feedback" technique they learned in sensitivity training. Some use a favorite theory of communication, or a theory in psychology such as positive reinforcement. Others quote a "Christian celebrity," or a quarterback, on ultimate matters of the soul! Further-more, the history of evangelism has not been entirely immune from the methods of manipulation, propaganda, and political coercion.

These sources and examples do not exhaust all ways to pursue evangelistic activity, but they do _show_ that a wide variety of sources exists, and such a laundry list at least suggests that the whole matter is worth thinking about. Why do Christians do what they do the way they do it? When we see that we have to stand on *some* source or follow *some* model, we are prepared to consider Church Growth as a source and model. I believe that, in an objective comparison with other sources for the practice of evangelism, the approach of Church Growth is compelling.

In Church Growth research, we find effectiveness in some of the approaches suggested above. We are particularly indebted to the growing body of intuitive or experientially derived lore found in good books on evangelism, such as *The Practice of Evangelism* by Bryan Green, *Effective Evangelism* by George Sweazey, *Pastoral Evangelism* by Samuel Southard, *Service Evangelism* by Richard Armstrong, or *Good News Is for Sharing,* by Leighton Ford.

But as a method for discovering what to do, Church Growth people believe that faithful, reproducing congregations are the laboratories of the living God. In such churches, the God who acts in history is showing his whole church the ways forward. Church Growth leaders believe that, through data collecting and case studies, we can discover the approaches and methods God is blessing to reach the undiscipled, and we may barely have scratched the surface. More reproducible principles and strategies are waiting to be discovered in churches already experiencing apostolic growth. Such research liberates Christian leaders from the myths of "magic," "mystery," and "modernity" (*see* Introductory) and teaches leaders how to cooperate effectively with the Great Commission.

The Church Growth "Package"

When you get involved with Church Growth, what is it that you are getting involved with? What commitments are involved? Is your commitment to the growth of your own church, or is it bigger than that? What are the dimensions of Church Growth? Church Growth sees God calling his church to grow in four distinct ways, which scholars call (1) Internal

Growth, (2) Expansion Growth, (3) Extension Growth, and
(4) Bridging Growth. Let us unpack that package and suggest
its importance.

Internal Growth refers to the growth in depth, quality, or
vitality of an already existing congregation. When the
nominal members discover the living Christ and begin
following him, when the members are more rooted in
scripture or more disciplined in prayer, when the people
become more loving or empowered, or more attuned to
God's will for peace and justice and finding the lost, then the
church is experiencing internal growth.

Expansion Growth is experienced when the church "ex-
pands" as new members join the flock. This category has
three strategic subdivisions: (a) When our own children come
up through the ranks and join, that is *biological* growth; (b)
when a family joins your church from another congregation
and you "send for their letter," that represents *transfer*
growth; (c) when persons who have not been active members
of a church discover Christ and join your church, that is
conversion growth.

Extension Growth occurs when a new local congregation is
"planted," usually to reach people that the "mother church"
would like to reach but cannot—because they are too far
away, geographically or culturally. Traditionally, extension
growth occurs when the mother church or judicatory buys
land, underwrites a founding pastor, and so forth. Increasingly, it also occurs when a church starts a second, third,
fourth, or fifth worshiping congregation in its present
facility. These are alternative congregations who speak a
different language or resonate to a different liturgical style.

Bridging Growth occurs when a church sends cross-cultural
missionaries across great cultural, linguistic, and (usually)
geographic barriers to communicate the gospel and establish
a church for a distinct group of people. There are still more
than two billion persons, and more than fifteen thousand
peoples, who have no cultural near-neighbors from whom
they are likely to receive the possibility of following Christ. So
the era for sending missionaries, as Yogi Berra says of a
baseball game, "isn't over until it's over!"

The Great Commission implies all four dimensions of

Church Growth, and healthy churches who have an apostolic consciousness and conscience pursue all four objectives. The four dimensions help us diagnose churches in trouble, and suggest ways forward.

For instance, the distinction between biological, transfer, and conversion growth helps us understand that the growth of many "growing" churches is soft, if not illusory. A decade ago, a Methodist church in a large Texas city was "leading our district in growth" and thought of itself as "a powerful evangelistic church." However, when the pastor analyzed his church's growth through Church Growth categories, he saw that more than 99 percent of the people received within the last two years represented biological or transfer growth. No longer harboring the illusion of being a great evangelistic church, they decided to become one and soon were receiving more than one hundred new Christians a year.

Again, some churches receive a lot of people into the membership, but virtually as many as are received become inactive. Analysis reveals a church with an interest in expansion growth, but not internal growth; they fail to "assimilate" their new people and, hence, limit the wider and deeper base that sustained expansion growth needs.

The opposite problem is more often found, that is, churches who are interested in internal growth but not in expansion growth, or at least "not yet." They desire to become a "better" church before they reach out, so they program renewal before outreach. But, what renews a stagnant church more reliably than a steady stream of new people into their ranks who have discovered Christ? Furthermore, how does a church become a "better church" without obeying God and becoming involved in apostolic ministry?

Once again, some churches study Church Growth, make bold plans, and launch new outreach—and no appreciable growth occurs! Why? Sometimes they have a commitment to their own internal and expansion growth, but not to extension and bridging growth. This means they are more interested in building their own institution than being instrumental in the salvation of all people, or, at best, they are interested in the redemption of people they can reach but not in the rest of humanity. Maybe God has perceived their dubious motives and has withheld his power and blessing from their outreach efforts!

The good news is that, for churches who "buy the whole package," more is now known about effectively delivering that package than any other generation has been privileged to know in the entire history of the Christian movement. This generation is perhaps more receptive to great news than any other. In this time of opportunity, God has not left his church intellectually abandoned. Many ways forward have been discovered, and in this second generation of Church Growth research and reflection, the most important principles may now be more integrated, coherent, and attainable.

Six "Mega-strategies"

We are now in a position to survey the themes of this book, in which we distill much of what can be known from Church Growth research and reflection into six general strategic principles. Undoubtedly, such an approach oversimplifies some complex matters and leaves some important things unsaid. However, this book is not written to satisfy purists, but to help a floundering church adopt and adapt ideas that, when understood and acted on, can make a great difference. McCabe's generation understood growth better than our own. That is why, after fifty years of proactive, confident extension-growth across a continent, the Methodists could sing

> "Extend," along the line is heard,
>   "Thy walls, O Zion fair!"
> And Methodism heard the word
>   And answers everywhere.
> A new church greets the morning's flame,
>   Another, evening's ray.
> "All hail the power of Jesus' name"—
>   We're building two a day!

1. Evangelizing people depends much more on God's grace, and on fluctuations in human responsiveness, than on

our precise theology and eloquence. Indeed, *churches grow as they learn how to identify and reach "receptive people"* whom God's prevenient grace has prepared to meet him. In every season, the Lord of the Harvest is bringing a "harvest" into being and is calling his church to lift up its eyes, and see where the fields are white for harvest. We now have from Church Growth research a body of valuable "indicators" for spotting receptive people, an immense aid to outreach in a mass society.

2. *Churches grow as they reach out across the social networks of their credible believers, especially their newest Christians.* The networks of Christians to their friends, relatives, neighbors, and colleagues give us what McGavran called "the bridges of God." Leaders can facilitate social network outreach in countless times and ways in the life of a congregation.

3. *Churches grow as they "multiply units" of various kinds* (classes, choirs, groups, congregations, et al.), *as recruiting groups and ports of entry for new persons.* New outreach units are the most prolific, and there is now no known theoretical limit to the membership strength a church can attain through the persistent expression of this principle.

4. *Churches grow as they minister to the felt needs of undiscipled people,* usually by developing new ministries. The last fifteen years have seen an immense rebirth of an entrepreneurial spirit within congregations. In any city today, you find ministries to blind people, singles, street people, immigrants, runaway kids, forgotten senior citizens, mentally handicapped adults, deaf people, unwed mothers, latchkey kids, handicapped children, dying and bereaved people, refugees, and a dozen or more other target populations. Yet the opportunities for compassionate service remain vast.

5. *Churches grow as they develop culturally indigenous ministries for the people they intend to reach.* Each people's culture is the medium of God's incarnational revelation to them. Furthermore, "indigenous ministry" is just as necessary to reach people "almost like us" as it is to reach a very different people with a different language. Churches with an indigenous strategy and ministries tend to be "contagious congregations."

6. *Churches grow from (prayerful) planning for their future,* deciding what future achievement they intend, laying the

stepping stones to get there, and implementing the plans. (This principle is not at all unique to Church Growth lore. Planning is behind the expansion and increased effectiveness of many kinds of organizations and institutions and has been conceptualized in the literature of management.)

Church Growth research has, in principle if not yet in practice, undermined some of Christian evangelicalism's more entrenched myths about how people ought to be reached and how the faith ought to spread. It will readily be seen that the six major principles, above, undermine six counterpart myths that have long frustrated the effectiveness of the Christian movement: (1) People are won when our evangelistic presentation is compelling; (2) People are usually evangelized by mature, theologically sophisticated Christian strangers; (3) The churches, worship services, classes, and groups our church already has ought to be able to reach all the winnable people; (4) A church grows by doing "its thing" and perpetuating the ministries it is used to; (5) The approach that won "us" (or that "turns me on") is the approach that ought to win "them"; (6) Churches grow as they wing it spiritually, responding spontaneously moment by moment to the Holy Spirit's leading. These six myths are variously phrased, and sometimes more assumed or implied than baldly stated, but their retarding influence upon the practice of evangelism is considerable. May this generation learn its way past them!

We can summarize the Church Growth strategies of this book in six words. Churches turn around and grow as they are:

1. *Identifying* receptive people to reach,
2. *Reaching* across social networks to people,
3. *Organizing* new recruiting groups and ports of entry,
4. *Ministering* to the needs of people,
5. *Indigenizing* ministries to fit the culture of the people, and
6. *Planning* to achieve the future they intend.

As people get into Church Growth, little happens at first. Indeed, "a little knowledge" may be "a dangerous thing," or at least a frustrating thing, like the Australian pastor's eighteen-legged cat. He explained: "She's got two forelegs, two fours are eight. Two hind legs, that's ten. Two on each side, that's fourteen. And, with one in each corner, that's eighteen legs!"

When people first get into Church Growth literature, they typically think they are meeting an eighteen-legged cat—because of Church Growth's many new terms, its multiple (and partly overlapping) principles, and its many cases from exotic places. However, say after three hundred hours of reading, rereading, reflecting, and teaching some of the ideas to others, one achieves a breakthrough and understands that Church Growth is only a four-legged cat after all. Now, one sees the principles of towering importance upon which the others depend. Through "Church Growth eyes," one sees a church and its community in ways one could not see them before. And with immersion knowledge of how Christianity spreads, one thinks like a strategist, sees the possibilities, and believes (with reason) that great things are possible and people can be reached. That is important, because we are involved with a self-fulfilling prophecy. If you believe that your outreach will attract people to faith, that belief increases the possibility that you *will* reach out, and it profoundly affects the *way* you reach out, and the very body language you use encourages the outcomes you expect.

The grassroots evangelists who attract people toward and into faith are the light of the world. They maintain clear objectives, are not easily deflected from them, and are assured of the validity of what they are doing and how they are doing it. They believe that God backs their efforts, that people will respond to care and truth, that the body of believers in the resurrected Christ will grow.

Such a man is Herman Thomas, who in 1941 was pastoring the Methodist church of Algoma, Wisconsin. One summer evening Thomas was visiting in a neighborhood by foot. His steps brought him to a home owned by one Robert G. Ingersol III, a brilliant engineer and grandson of the famous agnostic philosopher. The Ingersols had moved to Algoma a year before, and Mrs. Ingersol, a strong Christian, soon joined the church and sang in the choir. Ingersol visited occasionally.

Herman Thomas breathed a prayer for love and strength, and knocked on the door. Ingersol met him at the door, saying, "Pastor Thomas. I'm glad you've dropped by. I've been saving some questions for you." He posed his questions and seemed to appreciate the understanding and clarity of Thomas' replies. Then he asked, "Pastor Thomas, how can I become a follower of the Way? Will you help me?" Herman Thomas explained how the Spirit of Christ knocks at the heart's door, and how the person who opens the door will experience Christ's grace and will know he or she belongs to him. Thomas asked Ingersol if he would like to be led in a door-opening prayer to the Lord who knocks. "I would like that very much." They prayed, and Herman Thomas left knowing he had been the steward of a remarkable turning to God.

The next Sunday Ingersol came to church, walked forward during the singing of a hymn, and asked to be baptized into the community of the Messiah. Now the whole church was aware of this remarkable awakening.

One Sunday morning in 1942, the Algoma Methodist Church had another memorable service. Pastor Thomas baptized two infant boys into the Christian family. One was his own firstborn son. The other was a baby boy named Robert G. Ingersol IV! Had the church been silent in that moment, they would have heard some singing in the distance:

> We're building two a day, dear Bob,
>   We're building two a day!
> "All hail the power of Jesus' name,"
>   We're building two a day.

CHAPTER 2

John Wesley As Church Growth Strategist

The foundational conclusions from the Church Growth movement's first half century of research are as true as we thought, but not as new as we thought. Church Growth people have largely rediscovered what Christian history's greatest apostolic leaders knew and practiced (though the current body of lore is now more extensive than that of any one historical leader).

It is not fashionable to regard some of history's greatest Christian leaders as "strategists" who conceived, planned, led, and achieved "the impossible." We like to assume that God achieved great things like the exodus from Egypt or the evangelization of the Roman Empire through people who loved him with their hearts, but not with their minds! We like to regard historic Christian leaders as desk theologians, or church reformers, or parish preaching models, or models of spirituality, or as evangelists. However, some of them were also master strategists of powerful movements who planned great achievements, knew what they were doing, mobilized people and resources to attain their goals, and could show this generation how trails are blazed.

Our blindness reflects a wider conceit—which assumes that "strategy" is a twentieth-century discovery of, say, industrial barons, management gurus, and social movement leaders. When straining to find the way forward today, we do not often stand on the shoulders of Patrick, or Boniface, or William Carey to inform our cross-cultural missionary challenge. Nor do we learn from Augustine in preaching, or Francis in peacemaking, or Wilberforce and Garrison in seeking justice, or Charles G. Finney or John Wesley in evangelization. Wesley was, indeed, such a strategist, and his wisdom can illuminate today's Church Growth discussion.

To Spread the Power

John Wesley's unusual life-style is widely known and appreciated. He traveled by horse some 225,000 miles, preached 40,000 sermons, and survived hostile mobs and treacherous weather in carrying out his obsession. His achievements are almost as well known—perhaps 140,000 converts in his lifetime, the establishment of Methodism as an apostolic (and reform) movement within Anglicanism and, after his death, as a distinct church, the planting and care of a vast network of "classes" and "societies" governed by an annual "conference," and the outposting of the movement in North America.

But, more deeply, what did Wesley intend to achieve by all this activity? Some folks recall that Wesley wanted to "renew the church," and "spread scriptural holiness," and "reform the nation." But Wesley's more apostolic goals are not as widely recognized. He also, and even more basically, sought no less than the recovery of the truth, life, and power of earliest Christianity, and the expansion of that kind of Christianity. He singlemindedly managed the movement for fifty years by those objectives. He communicated these objectives to the growing ranks of Methodist people and leaders. He wrote and spoke frequently of the "increase," the "spread," and the "advancement" of this apostolic movement and believed that its expansion was expressing "the design of God." The movement's goal was to "save souls," which Wesley explains in "A Further Appeal to Men of Reason and Religion":

By salvation I mean, not barely, according to the vulgar notion, deliverance from hell, or going to heaven; but a present deliverance from sin, a restoration of the soul to its primitive health, its original purity; a recovery of the divine nature; the renewal of our souls after the image of God, in righteousness and true holiness, in justice, mercy and truth." (*The Works of John Wesley*, Vol. 8, p. 47)

For Wesley, the ministry of evangelism towered as a moral imperative: "We cannot with a good conscience neglect the present opportunity of saving souls while we live . . ." (*Works*, Vol. 8, p. 310). As the *apostolic* Protestant reformer, Wesley did not believe, as did Luther and Calvin, that the Great Commission was intended for the original apostles only. Rather, that Commission points the way for the whole church, in every generation, until all the peoples of the earth are reached. Accordingly, he taught his growing cadre of lay preachers that

you have nothing to do but to save souls. Therefore spend and be spent in this work. And go always, not only to those that want you, but to those that want you most.

Observe: It is not your business to preach so many times, and to take care of this or that society; but to save as many souls as you can; to bring as many sinners as you possibly can to repentance and with all your power to build them up in that holiness without which they cannot see the Lord. (*Works*, Vol. 8, p. 310)

Wesley regarded his growth objective for mission as no innovation. Indeed, he believed he had rediscovered the driving force of the earliest church. He championed basic "scriptural Christianity, as beginning to exist in individuals; as spreading from one to another; as covering the earth" (*Works*, Vol. 5, p. 38). He believed that the expansion of true faith is "the work of God"—an often used phrase that, he assures us, "is no cant word," but means "the conversion of sinners from sin to holiness," a work he saw as both "widening and deepening" (*Works*, Vol. 13, p. 329). He believed this work of God was so crucial that the leaders of Methodism in future generations must maintain a "single eye" in the service of its advancement.

This objective of the Methodist mission lodged in people's hearts through Charles Wesley's hymnody:

When He first the work begun,
Small and feeble was His Day:

41

Now the word doth swiftly run,
Now it wins its widening way.
                    (Quoted in Hildebrandt, 1956, p. 43)

Another Charles Wesley hymn reflects the extravagant hope
with which the early Methodists yearned for and expected
their movement's powerful growth:

    Savior, we know Thou art
        In every age the same;
    Now, Lord, in ours exert
        The virtue of Thy name;
    And daily, through Thy word increase
        Thy Blood-besprinkled witnesses.

    Thy people, saved below
        From every sinful stain,
    Shall multiply and grow
        If Thy command ordain;
    And one into a thousand rise,
        And spread Thy praise through earth and skies.

    In many a soul, and mine,
        Thou hast displayed Thy power;
    But to Thy people join
        Ten thousand thousand more,
    Saved from the guilt and strength of sin,
        In life and heart entirely clean.

A leader's motives relate, of course, to his or her objectives.
So, why would church leaders desire the growth of the
church? In his *Short History of the People Called Methodists*,
Wesley clarifies this issue for the Christian mission in all ages
and cultures: In traveling 4,000 to 5,000 miles a year by
horse, he now (1781) has company: "About a hundred and
thirty of my fellow-labourers are continually employed in the
same thing. We all aim at one point, (as we did from the hour
when we first engaged in the work), not at profit, any more
than at ease, or pleasure, or the praise of men; but to spread
true religion through London, Dublin, Edinburgh, and, as
we are able, through the three kingdoms" (*Works*, Vol. 8, pp.
380-81).

Charles Wesley "comprises in a few lines . . . the whole purpose of the brothers' mission" (Hildebrandt, 1956, p. 46, emphasis added):

> When first sent forth to minister the word,
> Say, did we preach ourselves, or Christ the Lord?
> Was it our aim disciples to collect,
> To raise a party, or to found a sect?
> No; but *to spread the power* of Jesus' name,
> Repair the walls of our Jerusalem
> Revive the piety of ancient days,
> And fill the earth with our Redeemer's praise.

And Hildebrandt reminds us in *Christianity According to the Wesleys,* that "evangelism, so understood, can never be the [exclusive] field of specialists or the target of extraordinary years and seasons in Methodism; it is the 'normal' work of the whole Church all the time—unless she has ceased, in truth and in deed, to be the Church of Christ" (1956, p. 46).

Sanctified Pragmatism

John Wesley informed an evangelistic movement with a sophistication that, perhaps, had not been seen for a thousand years. And his approach to informing the ministry of evangelism was remarkably close to that of today's Church Growth movement. For instance, he was an unapologetic pragmatist in the choice and development of strategies, models, and methods. The supreme standard for evaluating any evangelism approach was its outcomes, that is, whether or not the approach helped to achieve the perennial apostolic objectives of the discipling of people and the growth of the true Church. He wrote, "I would observe every punctilio or order, except when the salvation of souls is at stake. Then I prefer the end to the means" (quoted in Ensley, 1958, p. 39).

To be more specific, Wesley was a man of one book, the Bible, and from that book he received his message, the objectives of the mission, and the ethical guidelines for its expression; he would employ no approach prohibited by Scripture. But he parts company with other would-be restorers of primitive Christianity who try to imitate the forms and methods of the early church in its age and culture. Wesley developed or borrowed approaches that fit his target culture and were attended by God's clear blessing. He taught, in *A Plain Account of the People Called Methodists,* that "the Scripture, in most points, gives only general rules; and leaves the particular circumstances to be adjusted by the common sense of mankind" (*Works,* Vol. 8, p. 255). He did sometimes discover, as in Methodism's "class meetings," that "*without any design of so doing,* we have copied after another of the institutions of the Apostolic age" (*Works,* Vol. 8, p. 265, emphasis added).

Wesley probably came to this pragmatic stance through experience, consistent with his acceptance of experience as one source (with Scripture, tradition, and reason) of theological truth. For instance, in 1739 Wesley observed George Whitefield's experiment in field preaching to miners at Kingswood, near Bristol. In the first meeting Whitefield preached to about one hundred miners. By the fifth meeting, only a week later, he was addressing about ten thousand! The two men perceived the approach as a clear winner. They did not cast about for additional warrants, biblical or theological. Wesley's approach became so rigorously pragmatic that guidelines like the following appear to have shaped his practice:

1. If an approach or method ought to achieve your apostolic objectives, but does not, scuttle it—even if you like it!
2. If your employment of a method or approach is effective, use it to the hilt—even if you do not like it!
3. There is no perfect method which, like magic, will do the job for us. Rather, Christians evangelize, preceded and empowered by the Spirit, through culturally appropriate methods.

Wesley's bold pragmatism stands as a needed corrective to two widespread assumptions in today's ministry: (1) That I do what I enjoy, what "turns me on" and gives vocational satisfaction, even if it is not effective; and (2) that I refrain from doing anything that "turns me off" or with which I am not "comfortable," even if it is effective. Robert Tuttle tells me that Wesley sometimes challenged his people: "If you don't like [field preaching], learn to like it!" Some people are too easily "turned off," and one's comfort or enjoyment level may have little to do with the validity of any ministry. Indeed, the test of our faithfulness may be our willingness to employ a demonstrably effective method that we may not enjoy.

Both Wesleys passed this test, thus making possible a contagious movement. Charles was a cultured poet and musician with high church aesthetic tastes, but he shelved his preferences, condescending to write hymns to the tunes of lowbrow drinking songs being sung in England's public houses! And John, after thirty-three years of open-air field preaching to the unchurched, confessed that "to this day field preaching is a cross to me. But I know my commission and see no other way of 'preaching the gospel to every creature' " (*Journal*, September 6, 1772).

Strategy from Research

Wesley's pragmatism corresponds remarkably to today's Church Growth movement. Wesley's approach to evangelism and the movement's spread was even "research based," employing rudimentary versions of what became qualitative behavioral science research methods. Methodist tradition has long been clear that Wesley developed much of Methodism's understanding of pastoral ministry through practical field research (*see* Martin Schmidt, Vol. 2, part two, 1973, ch. 8), but to my knowledge the tradition has not adequately perceived how Wesley's field research methods informed Methodism's wider evangelism and growth.

For instance, Wesley practiced rigorous *observation.* His power for observing crowds (even while preaching) astonishes. He observed classes, societies, towns, hecklers and detractors, leaders, parish churches, persons and crowds, and others. He also gathered data through thousands of *interviews* with local Methodist leaders, converts, new Methodists, local opinion leaders, people with needs, and others.

He welcomed, received, and solicited *reports* from Methodist leaders from across the movement.

Over the years Wesley *recorded,* in a *Journal,* his observations and what he learned from others from interviews and reports. These recorded studies stretched into multiple volumes. He *reviewed* his journal from time to time, to assimilate the data, to analyze trends in various towns and regions, to perceive where people were becoming more responsive, to prepare for return visits, to make midcourse corrections, to map itineraries, to inform strategy. Wesley took data seriously, and on crucial matters he took no one's word, but checked on the accuracy of data himself. Recounting his 1748 visit to Dublin, his journal states,

I inquired into the state of the society. Most pompous accounts had been sent me, from time to time, of the great numbers that were added to it; so that I confidently expected to find therein six or seven hundred members. And how is the real fact? I left three hundred and ninety-four members; and I doubt if there are now three hundred and ninety-six! (March 16, 1748)

I returned to Norwich, and took an exact account of the society. I wish all our preachers would be accurate in their accounts, and rather speak under than above the truth. I had heard again and again of the increase of the society. And what is the naked truth? Why, I left it 202 members; and I find 179. (March 21, 1779)

Wesley's research was intended to answer such basic questions as the causes of growth, decline, and stagnation in churches. At times he employs a McGavran-like *historical analysis,* discerning causes of both growth and decline by using the ups and downs of a graph of growth to dig out the reasons. For instance, in his journal entry of October 12, 1764, he records available membership data on the recent history of the puzzling and mercurial Norwich society, which can be tabled (or graphed).

Year	Members
1755	83
1757	134
1758	110

1759	760
1760	507
1761	412
1762	630
1763	310
1764	174

As Wesley reflected on his data, his powerful inductive mind built up an impressive body of causes, barriers, and explanations for the Methodist movement's trends. For instance, in *A Short History of the People Called Methodists,* he offers a lucid analysis of a crucial issue in early Methodism—the typical pyramidal response to field preaching.

But how is it, that almost in every place, even where there is no lasting fruit, there is so great an impression made at first upon a considerable number of people? The fact is this: Everywhere the work of God rises higher and higher, till it comes to a point. Here it seems for a short time to be at a stay; and then it gradually sinks again.

All this may easily be accounted for. At first, curiosity brings many hearers; at the same time, God draws many by his preventing grace to hear his word, and comforts them in hearing. One then tells another. By this means, on the one hand, curiosity spreads and increases; and, on the other, the drawings of God's Spirit touches more hearts, and many of them more powerfully than before. He now offers grace to all that hear, most of whom are in some measure affected, and, more or less moved with approbation of what they hear, have a desire to please God, with good-will to his messenger. And these principles, variously combined and increasing, raise the general work to its highest point. But it cannot stand here, in the nature of things. Curiosity must soon decline. Again, the drawings of God are not followed, and thereby the Holy Spirit is grieved: He strives with this and that man no more, and so His drawings end. Thus, the causes of the general impression declining, most of the hearers will be less and less affected. Add to this, that, in process of time, 'it must be that offenses will come.' Some of the hearers, if not Teachers also, will act contrary to their profession. Either their follies or faults will be told from one to another, and lose nothing in the telling. Men, once curious to hear, will hear no more; men, once drawn, having stifled their good desires, will disapprove what they approved of before, and feel dislike instead of good-will to the Preachers. Others who were more or less convinced, will be afraid or ashamed to acknowledge that conviction; and all these will catch at ill stories, true or false, in order to justify their change. When, by that means, all who do not savingly believe have quenched the Spirit of God, the little flock that remain go on from faith to faith; the rest sleep and take their rest; and thus the number of hearers in every place may be expected, first to increase, and then to decrease. (*Works,* Vol. 13, pp. 338-39)

On Growth and Quality

Mr. Wesley brings needed depth and perspective to a current controversy in the church, a discussion on the relation between "quantity" and "quality" in church membership strength. One camp insists on "the more members the better," that an increasing membership correlates with greater quality of church life and faithfulness. The other camp, in a version of "remnant" theory, insists that a church gets better as it gets smaller, that quantity and quality are inversely correlated.

Mr. Wesley, for the most part, sides with the first camp and challenges the second. Some cases may support the quality-through-decline thesis; his journal even records one such case in his first twelve years of itineration and analysis, (the society in metropolitan Mount-Mellick, Ireland, May 26, 1750). However, Wesley observed that normally, as a church grows it becomes stronger and better, and as a church declines it becomes weaker and less healthy. He also found a correlation between growth and depth: The societies in which members thirsted for and expected their own sanctification were also experiencing growth. To be sure, Wesley had no interest in *puffed* statistics and he tolerated no "numbers games." In reflecting on a case of the society in Dublin, he interpreted it as "a warning to us all, how we give in to that hateful custom of painting things beyond the life. Let us make a conscience of magnifying or exaggerating any thing. Let us rather speak under, than above, the truth. We, of all men, should be punctual in what we say; that none of our words may fall to the ground" (*Journal,* March 16, 1748).

His 1761 observation of the work at Bristol notes the correlation of membership growth and of quality growth, typical of many such observations: "Here likewise I had the satisfaction to observe a considerable increase in the work of

God. The congregations were exceedingly large, and the people hungering and thirsting after righteousness; and every day afforded us fresh instances of persons converted from sin, or converted to God" (*Journal*, October 1, 1761).

To be sure, Wesley perceived problems in the experiences of growing Methodist societies. For instance, in London "I found the work of God swiftly increasing here . . . Meantime, the enemy was not wanting in his endeavors to sow tares among the good seed. I saw this clearly, but durst not use violence, lest, in plucking up the tares, I should root up the wheat also" (*Journal*, August 22, 1761). In cases where the tares took over or had pathological influence in a society, Wesley knew and exercised appropriate interventions, frequently including the removal of unfaithful or unserious members from membership. But Wesley saw that declining churches and societies have problems too, and his wide experience persuaded him that the problems connected with growth were far preferable. He knew that, in any major change, a church is trading one set of problems for another set of problems. What matters is whether the church is trading up or down. Wesley's experience convinced him that, in the vast majority of cases, a growing society is trading up—and getting a better set of problems; a declining society is trading down and getting a tragic set of problems.

Mr. Wesley strongly preferred growth to decline, and saw that quality and depth typically accompany growth, because God is at work in "the work of God": "I observed God is reviving his work in Kingswood: The society, which had been much decreased, being now increased again to near three hundred members; many of whom are now athirst for full salvation, which for some years they had almost forgot" (*Journal*, October 11, 1761). Evangelism efforts need God's blessing and power for church growth to take place:

In the afternoon I preached at Alemouth. How plain an evidence have we here, that even our outward work, even the societies are not of man's building! With all our labour and skill, we cannot, in nine years time, form a society in this place; even though there is none that opposes, poor or rich. Nay, though the two richest men in town, and the only gentlemen there, have done all in their power to further it. (*Journal*, May 15, 1752)

Wesley observed that, at different times and places, God varies his work. He observed in Bristol in 1740 that the work of God "last Spring . . . poured along like a rapid flood, overwhelming all before him." Whereas now,

> He deigns his influence to infuse,
> Secret, refreshing as the silent dews.

Furthermore, sometimes the stream is wider, sometimes deeper (*Journal,* November 18, 1742). But whatever its shape and pace, a society's growth signifies God's power and the church's vitality: "I began speaking severally to the members of the society, and was well pleased to find so great a number of them much alive to God. One consequence of this, is, that the society is larger than it has been for several years: And no wonder, for where the real power of God is, it naturally spreads wider and wider (*Journal,* April 7, 1760).

It is appropriate to qualify Wesley's enthusiasm for growth. He championed the growth of the "true church," defined not in doctrinaire terms, but by the teaching of the apostles' gospel, by the people's faith, love, and discipline, and by their desire for social reform and full salvation from sin's power. So Wesley would not celebrate, today, the mere statistical growth of any company that calls itself a church. Extending the New Testament's analogy of the church to a body, Wesley would agree that some growth is not desirable, like the growth in a person's body that is malignant or mere fat.

But Wesley rejoices wherever he finds that "the word of God runs indeed; and loving faith spreads on every side" (*Works,* Vol. 12, p. 122). He perceived a society's membership decline as a "sore evil" needing "remedy" (*Works,* Vol. 13, p. 329). In much of his itinerant ministry, he analyzed struggling or declining societies and he applied the needed "remedies." Furthermore, Wesley defended Methodism's very right to exist by pointing to its growth. In a challenging letter to the Anglican Bishop of Exeter, he asks: "When hath religion, I will not say, since the Reformation, but since the time of Constantine the Great, made so large a progress in any nation, within so short a space?" (*Works,* Vol. 9, p. 22). And in 1777 he observed that,

In most places, the Methodists are still a poor despised people, labouring under reproach and many inconveniences; therefore, where the power of God is not, they decrease. By this then you may form a sure judgment. Do the Methodists in general decrease in number? Then they decrease in grace; they are fallen, or, at least, a falling people. But they do not decrease in number; they continually increase. Therefore, they are not a fallen people. (*Journal*, May 8, 1777)

To Receptive People

As the strategic leader of Methodism, John Wesley anticipated most of the major universal "mega-strategies" that I have identified from existing Church Growth research. He strongly practiced and advanced three of them, and taught them to other Methodist leaders.

Wesley observed that "the Lord of the Harvest" is almost continuously moving among some people to prepare a "harvest" for his church to gather. He thereby discovered the principle of priority outreach to receptive people while it is "harvest time." He pursued the principle even more avidly than McGavran. For Wesley and the early Methodists, there were always "fields white unto harvest," because in every season the Holy Spirit (by his "prevenient grace") moved through the events and circumstances of some people's lives to open their hearts to the gospel. Wesley learned to perceive whether people were hostile, resistant, indifferent, interested, or receptive. Even before his 1738 "heart strangely warmed" experience at Aldersgate Street, which assured him of his justification and empowered him for apostolic ministry, Wesley had attempted to communicate the Christian religion to American Indians in Georgia but came home—"There being no possibility, as yet, of instructing the Indians; neither had I, as yet, found or heard of any Indians on the continent of America who had the least desire of being instructed" (*Journal*, October 30, 1737). So he learned early to appreciate, and respond to, receptive people wherever he found them. He also learned to withdraw from resistant fields and spend more energy where there was harvest to be gathered.

Of course, Wesley sometimes "looked a mob in the face" and ministered to other resistant populations. He knew that people are "softened by degrees," so by design he intentionally planted seeds that would later flower into an openness to the gospel. He knew that, like flowers, people do not remain open forever. He thereby discovered a new source of evangelistic urgency—reaching receptive people while they are receptive, lest we miss the day of their visitation.

The receptivity principle informed his practice and his itinerary. In the cities, he reached out to the receptive new urban working peoples more than to resistant longtime urban dwellers. In the countryside, mining peoples were more receptive than farming peoples. The people of the South of England were less receptive than those of the North—"where one Preacher is increased into seven" (*Works*, Vol. 12, p. 309). But in the South, Bristol, Cornwall, and some of the populations of London also proved receptive. Wesley knew (as McGavran would rediscover) that "the masses" are generally more receptive than "the classes." Furthermore, Wesley knew why this *had* to be so: "I preached at Hadding-ton, in Provost D's yard, to a very elegant congregation. But I expect little good will be done here, for we begin at the wrong end: *religion must not go from the greatest to the least, or the power would appear to be of men*" (*Journal*, May 21, 1764, emphasis added).

But he saw receptivity expand upward in his lengthy career. By 1766 he could observe that

the fields in every part of England are indeed white for the harvest. There is everywhere an amazing willingness in the people to receive either instruction or exhortation. We find this temper now even in many of the higher rank, several of whom cared for none of these things. But surely the time is coming for these also; for the scripture must be fulfilled, "They shall all know me, from the least even to the greatest." (*Works*, Vol. 12, p. 192)

As Mr. Wesley reviewed his journal entries on a city or town and studied more recent reports, he estimated where receptivity was high, or increasing, and planned his schedule strategically. But a schedule was negotiable. When a town was less receptive than expected, he could shake the dust of that town off his feet and move on earlier than planned. When he discovered a town was more receptive than expected, he might stay longer than originally planned. For example, he records in his journal (May 9, 1781): "I preached . . . in the evening at Shrewsbury, where, seeing the earnestness of the people, I agreed to stay another day." He could also make strategic adjustments on the spot. In Rochdale (October 18, 1747):

As soon as ever we entered the town, we found the streets lined on both sides with multitudes of people, shouting, cursing, blaspheming, and gnashing upon us with their teeth. Perceiving it would not be practical to preach abroad, I went into a large room, open to the street, and called aloud "Let the wicked forsake his way, and the unrighteous man his thoughts."

Wesley taught the Methodists to identify and reach out to receptive people. This strategy became a standard principle of Methodist evangelization. Excerpts from the *Minutes of Several Conversations Between the Reverend Mr. Wesley and Others* are especially memorable:

Q. Where should we endeavor to preach the most?
A. 1. Where there is the greatest number of quiet and willing hearers.
2. Where there is most fruit . . .
Q. Ought we not diligently to observe in what places God is pleased at any time to pour out his Spirit more abundantly?
A. We ought; and at that time to send more labourers than usual into that part of the harvest. (*Works*, Vol. 13, pp. 300-301)

Indigenous Ministries

From their pragmatic philosophy, the Wesley brothers developed an "indigenous" approach to ministry more than a century before anthropologists could tell us what to call it. Wesley knew that a people's culture is the medium of God's revelation to them. He sensed that when the cultural form of ministry "fits" the people, they have the best chance to understand and respond. The Wesleys did not act on this principle without *kenosis*, or self-emptying, of their own "Oxbridge" cultural tastes. However, they felt called to reach the working peoples of England, who never went to church, whom the established church had written off. The Wesleys demonstrated that forms of outreach that "fit" a people make it more possible for them to respond than do alien or "superior" cultural forms.

So Wesley, and other Methodist preachers, typically engaged these unreached pagans in the open air, on their turf—perhaps in a market square, or a church yard, or a park, or a wide city street, or a crossroads, or beside a mine, or a natural amphitheater. The approach became known as "field preaching." "I could scarcely reconcile myself at first to this strange way of preaching in the fields . . . I had been all my life (till very lately) so tenacious of every point relative to decency and order that I should have thought the saving of souls almost a sin if it had not been done in a church" (*Journal,* March 31, 1749).

As an astute student of rhetoric, Wesley considered the role of effective language in public communication, and he championed language with transparent meaning for the target audience. He attempted to rivet this value into *The Character of a Methodist:*

The distinguishing marks of a Methodist are not his opinions of any sort . . . But as to all opinions which do not strike at the root of Christianity, we think and let think . . .

Neither are words or phrases of any sort. We do not place our religion, or any part of it, in being attached to any peculiar mode of speaking, any quaint or uncommon set of expressions. The most obvious, easy, common words, wherein our meaning can be conveyed, we prefer before others, both on ordinary occasions, and when we speak of the things of God. We never, therefore, willingly or designedly, deviate from the most usual way of speaking; unless when we express scripture truths in scripture words, which, we presume, no Christian will condemn. (*Works,* Vol. 8, p. 340)

The Christian communicator today, of course, has access to more indigenous translations of the Bible than had eighteenth-century Methodists, eliminating that one qualifier in Wesley's principle of clarity. Translations such as the Good News Bible now fit "the most usual way of speaking" and there is, or should be, no longer any distinction between "Bible language" and ordinary language at its best. Today, no Christian has any legitimate excuse for masking Christian truth in antiquated or stained-glass language.

Wesley also warned Methodists against "refining" the Christianity they had received—which he saw as an inevitable temptation in Christians who experience what McGavran calls "redemption and lift." From the consciousness-raising and self-developing experiences within the Christian community, people experience raised self-esteem, literacy and education, increased aspirations, and sometimes greater prosperity or upward mobility. With all this comes, typically, some embarrassment about one's roots and some reach for greater "sophistication." Wesley, though learned himself, took a dim view of self-conscious sophistication and especially of new theologies that presume to improve on classical Christianity. He declared that "to refine religion is to spoil it" (*Works,* Vol. 13, p. 165).

We have seen that Charles Wesley wrote an extensive indigenous hymnody for England's common people, an achievement of enduring Methodist pride, though not a unique achievement. Indeed, Eugene Nida reminds us that "*all* creative and extensive periods of church growth have been characterized by an appropriate indigenous hymnody" (quoted in "Dynamics of Church Growth," 1976, p. 182, emphasis added).

Wesley, in addition, developed the tract and the (somewhat longer) pamphlet as indigenous forms of getting the Word out to people and instruction to the Methodists. Eighteenth-century Methodism published and circulated many of Wesley's essays, such as his "Earnest Appeal to Men of Reason and Religion," "A Plain Account of the People Called Methodists," "The Character of a Methodist," "A Short History of Methodism," "Advice to the People Called Methodists," "The Principles of a Methodist," the published "Conversations," and the later "Short History of the People Called Methodists." Such writings were foundational in Methodist minds of the eighteenth-century, a period in which most leaders were immersed in the principles behind the movement's expansion.

Methodism also published thousands of tracts, which were widely distributed. Wesley worked to inculcate a redundant communication strategy involving the tracts. He advised traveling preachers to carry tracts and books on some particular subject in a given preaching round, to preach in that round on that subject, and "after preaching, encourage the congregation to buy and read the tract." On the next round, they were to preach and make tracts available on another subject, and so on (*Works*, Vol. 12, p. 320).

As an indigenous communicator, Wesley came to experience that identification with the target population that anthropologists tell us is crucial for communication in any cultural setting and in the diffusion of any new idea, cause, or technology. From Newcastle, Wesley tells us, "The people in all these parts are much alive to God, being generally plain, artless, and simple of heart. Here I should spend the greatest part of my life, if I were to follow my own inclinations. But I am not to do my own will, but the will of Him that sent me" (*Works*, Vol. 12, p. 177).

Multiplication of Units

John Wesley pioneered and mastered the Church Growth principle called today (for want of a better generic term) "the multiplication of units." He was instrumental in spawning many hundreds of classes, bands, societies, and other groups with distinct agendas, and he labored to develop the indigenous lay leadership that this growing vast network of groups would need. He was driven to multiplying "classes," for these served best as recruiting groups, as ports of entry for new people, and for involving awakened people with the gospel and its power. Much of his entire strategy can be summarized in four maxims:

1. Preach and visit in as many places as you can.
2. Go most where they want you most.
3. Start as many classes as can be effectively managed.
4. Do *not* preach where you cannot enroll awakened people in classes.

One can see how important class multiplication was in Wesley's strategy by observing how he concluded a field preaching session. Seldom (if ever) did he invite people to accept Christ and become Christians on the spot.

How *did* Wesley conclude an open air session? Sometimes he announced that he would remain for those who wanted to converse personally. Often, to test the actual receptivity of apparently interested people, he announced a service the next morning at five o'clock! Most often, he invited people to join a class—sometimes a new class that would meet that evening. Then he explained the one condition that a person had to meet to join a class—to express the desire "to flee the wrath to come," to know God's acceptance, and to live a higher life (*see* Wood, 1967, ch. 14).

An entourage sometimes traveled with Wesley, and during open air services they scattered among the crowd, studying faces, conversing with individuals, and inviting them to join a class. The first objective in much of the field preaching was the starting of classes.

Wesley's rationale for this practice is rooted in his understanding of the process, by stages, in which people become Christians, and upon which he based his whole practice of evangelism. In brief, he believed that you

1. Awaken people—to the fact of their lostness, their sins, their need for God.
2. Enroll awakened people in a class (and, in three months, in a Methodist society). Their experiences within class and society will keep them awake and prepare them for their justification and new birth.
3. Teach awakened enrolled people to expect to experience their justification. They would experience, at a time and in a manner of God's choosing, his forgiveness and acceptance.
4. Teach justified people to expect to experience their sanctification in this life. Christians can expect God's grace to complete the work begun in their justification. His grace will free their hearts from sin's power so that their lives can be motivated by love and nothing else.

This four-stage process is consistent with his theological design (which Albert Outler refers to as Wesley's "Ordo Salutis"). In Wesleyan evangelism, each stage served as a conscious *objective* to be achieved in people's lives. In the cases of unchurched pagans, these four objectives were achieved in the 1, 2, 3, 4 sequence suggested above. In the cases of second or third generation nominal Methodists, we find many examples of people who are (1) already members of a class and a society but who need (2) to be awakened, (3) justified, and (4) made whole in love. So in time part of the mission field was to be found inside Methodism's membership.

In eighteenth-century Methodism's evangelical ministry, the ministries of field preaching and Christian witnessing pursued the first two objectives: (1) to awaken people, and (2) to enroll awakened people in a "class," that is, a lay-led redemptive cell. From the experiences of the class meeting, most of the awakened people experienced, in time, acceptance and reconciliation to God; and some of the justified people, in time, experienced the completion of the work God began in their acceptance.

To Wesley, evangelism (in the sense of the spiritual "obstetrics" that makes new birth possible) took place primarily in the class meetings and in people's hearts in the hours following class meetings. In part, this strategy was a concession to Wesley's own limits, since he was not a great "obstetrician-evangelist." He was a great apologist, and a great awakener, but not quite a great evangelist. For instance, Charles brought more people into faith than John, but John started far more people toward faith. And, in part, Wesley put most of his fertile eggs in the class-meeting basket because he had experienced, from his mother onward, the contagious power of devout laity and lay-led cells. Besides, as in Lord Soper's dictum, Wesley believed that Christianity is "more caught than taught." Wesley also observed that awakening people without folding them into redemptive cells does more harm than good! In a journal entry of 1743 he declares, "The devil himself desires nothing more than this, that the people of any place should be half-awakened and then left to themselves to fall asleep again. Therefore, I determine by the grace of God not to strike one stroke in any place where I cannot follow the blow." Twenty years later, the principle had become even more resolute:

I was more convinced than ever that the preaching like an apostle without joining together those that are awakened and training them up in the ways of God, is only begetting children for the murderer . . . How much preaching has there been for these twenty years all over Pembrokeshire. But no regular societies, no discipline, no order or connection; and the consequence is that nine in ten of the once awakened are now faster asleep than ever. (*Journal,* August 25, 1763)

In the *Minutes of Several Conversations,* Mr. Wesley is asked:

Q. Is it advisable for us to preach in as many places as we can, without forming any societies?
A. By no means. We have made the trial in various places; and that for a considerable time. But all the seed has fallen as by the highway side. There is scarce any fruit remaining. (*Works,* Vol. 8, p. 300)

Frontiers

John Wesley was, of course, much more than a "church growth guru." At the same time, he understandably lacked the completeness of a twentieth-century Church Growth scholar or movement theorist. He lacked access to our more refined behavioral science research methods, and to the knowledge now available from the applied behavioral sciences. He lacked access to our extensive data, today's hundreds of published case studies, and today's wide community of scholars in evangelization and church growth.

So while he anticipated some Church Growth strategies with remarkable clarity and force, he only glimpsed other major Church Growth principles. For instance, his *Journal* occasionally observes the role of acquaintances, spouses, friends, parents, and others in bringing undiscipled persons to meetings, and so forth, but he did not conceptualize, emphasize, or teach anything like McGavran's social network strategy for outreach.

Again, Wesley was much engaged in ministry to persons, focusing especially on their needs and struggles, and occasionally he launched new ministries such as the school at Kingswood, but he lacked access to the kinds of marketing models and the methods for researching and serving discrete "markets" that our society takes for granted. Also, Wesley was probably mistaken in his occasional advocacy of field preaching as something like a universally necessary and effective model for engaging the unchurched.

Yet he knew "more" than we do today. He employed some principles in guiding Methodism's expansion that "modern" Church Growth people have yet to probe sufficiently: (1) The four-stage process corresponding to his "Order of Salvation" has its own integrity and obvious effectiveness in evangelistic ministry. (2) His goal for people, that they turn toward Christ *and* "be made perfect in love in this life," is deeply worth ecumenical consideration. (3) As in his *Advice to the People Called Methodists*, Wesley would warn all Christians not to practice any kind of coercive evangelism: "Abhor every approach, in any kind or degree, to the spirit of persecution. If you cannot reason or persuade a man into the truth, never attempt to force him into it. If love will not compel him to come in, leave him to God, the Judge of all" (*Works*, Vol. 12, p. 201).

(4) Wesley would probably challenge today's "comity" arrangements in missions and interchurch relations, arrangements in which, say, the Methodists do not reach out to Native Americans of the Dakotas because historically the government assigned the Dakotas to the Episcopalians (who aren't doing anything!). It would remind him of the Anglican Church's counterproductive "parish" system and of the time he was scolded for "preaching in another man's parish." Wesley believed that *all* church policies and structures should be judged by whether they facilitate or frustrate "the work of God" and the "spread of true religion." He saw the parish system as frustrating the Great Commission, and therefore declared that, as one called into apostolic ministry, "I look upon all the world as my parish" (*Journal*, June 11, 1739).

(5) Wesley would have the ordination standards for clergy serve the apostolic mission of the church. Indeed, the church's whole organization is supposed to serve that mission. He used four criteria for discerning the persons who "are moved by the Holy Ghost" to enter vocational ministry: (a) "Do they know God?" (b) "Have they gifts?" (c) "Have they the graces?" (d) "Have they fruit? Are any truly convinced of sin, and converted to God, by their preaching?" Modern

Methodist conferences generally take the first for granted, and have eliminated the fourth, thereby adding many to the clergy who are, at best, competent chaplains for people who are already Christians. Furthermore, Wesley would remind us that, when Methodism was a contagious movement, the preachers were strategically appointed to advance the apostolic goals of the movement and *not* essentially to be rewarded through advancements or better parsonages.

(6) Wesley, as a student of rhetoric, was aware of how vital is the "ethos" and credibility of preachers and laity in the spread of faith. It matters, supremely, that Christians live by the faith they commend, that they understand it, are growing in it, and feel compassionate good will for the lost who have not found the Way. Among his dozens of allusions to this principle, his "short method" for the conversion of Ireland is most memorable. He declared there to be "one way" to achieve this bold proposal,

and one only; one that will (not probably, but) infallibly succeed. If this way is taken, I am willing to stake my life upon the success of it. And it is a plain, simple way . . .

Here, therefore, is the short and sure method. Let all the clergy of the Church of Ireland only live like the Apostles, and preach like the Apostles, and the thing is done. (*Works*, Vol. 10, p. 130)

John Wesley, as one apostolic genius of the Christian past, offers still more strategic gold to this generation's confused church. He reminds us that many wheels do not have to be reinvented, and that we may stand on the shoulders of the achievers of the past and rediscover lost pieces of the "communion of the saints." And he is no narrow, sectarian Methodist; his "catholic spirit" affirmed, celebrated, and would advance every Christian tradition.

The worth of John Wesley's published church growth ideas is demonstrated in Methodism's experience. British Methodism's period of greatest growth came in the generation after Wesley's death—a generation with him no longer at the helm, but one in which the leaders were steeped in his normative writings and ideas. Wesley had few (if any) church growth secrets. In his voluminous writing he shared, piecemeal, virtually everything he knew.

Wesley's wide publication of church growth principles enabled Francis Asbury to immigrate to America and duplicate Wesley's achievement in the new country. Indeed, at the time of Wesley's death, American Methodism had already grown to the strength of British Methodism. Though Asbury is commonly thought of as Wesley's "apprentice," there is no evidence of any extensive tutorial relationship. His achievement in North America was possible because Asbury became "possessed of Mr. Wesley's writing, and for some years almost laid aside all other books but the Bible, and applied himself exceedingly closely in reading every book that Mr. Wesley had written" (quoted in Baker, 1976, p. 116). Indeed, Asbury's sophisticated grasp of Wesley's ideas enabled him to adapt them strategically to the different challenge the American mission field presented.

The day for John Wesley's strategic wisdom is not over, for many of his principles have perennial validity. As Wesley the "strategic genius" is rediscovered, he will become one of the strategic fountainheads of the Christian movement facing the twenty-first century.

Identifying
Receptive People

We have explored the origins of the modern Church Growth movement in the research approach of Donald McGavran, employing historical analysis, observation, questionnaires, and interviews to discover principles behind Christianity's expansion. We have suggested that John Wesley was a predecessor of McGavran who also gathered data, reflected on it, and generated principles, and that these principles were widely taught and informed Methodism's expansion. Wesley's legacy provides roots and depth for Church Growth thought in this century and the next.

We have also suggested that, after fifty years, it is possible to unpack much of Church Growth's strategic insight in ways that are more readily useful. The remaining six chapters will propound six "mega-strategies" that, when understood, assimilated, taught in the church, and repeatedly acted upon, will typically result in the sustained growth of established churches within a society.

These six major principles presuppose that certain features of a church's people and leaders are essentially in place: That they want to reach people and are willing to pay the price; that they are primarily motivated by gratitude for grace experienced, obedience to the Great Commission, and compassion for lost people needing to be found, and not by thoughts of success, career advancement, or empire building; that they are open to the Spirit's power and leadership and are not escaping into overreliance on knowledge or technology; that they are passionately committed to Christ's mission throughout the world and to becoming a biblical, faithful, contagious church. It is also assumed that the readers are serious enough in their stewardship of the gospel to want to learn "the trade," not merely "the tricks of the trade"; leaders need to *understand* principles to use them appropriately and effectively.

The first mega-strategy is Church Growth's most remarkable contribution to informed evangelization: the principle of *receptivity*. Using common sense, we may observe that some people are more receptive to the gospel than others, and that a given person is more receptive now than last year. What is more, McGavran discovered that whole populations swing back and forth around all or part of an imaginary axis—from hostility to resistance, to indifference, to interest, to receptivity—and some people are always found at each point on that axis.

The good news is that in every season some people and groups are receptive. They have been prepared for "harvest" by the Lord of the Harvest, and the church's greatest apostolic opportunity in any season is to identify and reach the receptive people while they are receptive. Today, the power of Jesus' name is spreading in many lands and peoples because missionary leaders and national leaders, schooled in Church Growth principles, have identified societies and population groups "ripe unto harvest."

The New Testament church viewed the world through these strategic lenses. They believed that God prepares certain "harvests" of people, and he wants his laborers to gather those harvests (Luke 10:2). Some people are like the "good soil," in which the seed of God's Word is planted, takes root, grows, and multiplies. The Lord's imperative is to let those people hear who have the ears to hear (Mark 4:9). Jesus counseled those who spread the gospel to shake the dust of resistant towns off their feet and hurry to towns more receptive to the message of the inbreaking reign of God (Luke 9:5).

The book of Acts reflects this strategy in action as Paul, in many towns, first reaches out to the "godfearers," Gentile co-travelers of the synagogues who had accepted Judaism's one God and her scriptures, but had remained Gentile culturally—that is, they had not given up pork, or submitted to the rigor of adult circumcision, or adopted many other Jewish customs. Paul found the godfearers, typically, to be a city's most receptive group. He presented the gospel as continuous with what they now believed and as fulfilling their own culture, not requiring them to leave it. They frequently became the core group of the new church in their city. The new church then reached out across their social networks, house churches multiplied and received more new people, and by the synergistic effect of church growth principles working together the new church grew.

People "Ripe for the Gospel"

John Wesley grasped the principle of receptivity, saw its importance in evangelization, and taught it to Methodism. The supreme opportunity is always people who are "ripe for the gospel," meaning that "they are earnestly desirous of being instructed in it; and [usually] as utterly ignorant of it they are, as any Creek or Cherokee Indians" (*Journal,* October 30, 1739). Early in his ministry, he had not found the American Indians to be receptive, but back in England and after Aldersgate, Wesley found many receptive people; or rather, he had now learned to identify receptive people and to discern signs of receptivity. Indeed, whereas Wesley's old problem was in finding any receptive American Indians, his new problem became the identification of more harvest than his movement had the human resources, in number or competency, to gather (*Works,* Vol. 12, pp. 188-89). To a Mr. Hopper, Wesley laments: "We want more labourers; especially in the North, where one Preacher is increased into seven! and the people cry aloud for more. But alas! we can neither make them, nor hire them" (*Works,* Vol. 12, p. 309).

A comparison of the resistance Mr. Wesley found in America and the receptivity he found in England says more about the change in Wesley's perception of fields for mission than it says about either field. While Wesley and his people were gathering a harvest in England, most of the Church of

England neither gathered harvest nor saw it. Meanwhile, Asbury and others found extensive opportunity to expand the faith in the colonies, including some Indian tribes. This harvest was, again, overlooked or denied by the Episcopalians in the colonies. Wesley and the other Methodists had received what McGavran calls "church growth eyes." They were now able to perceive harvests that they were formerly blind to, that others were still blind to.

Where do "church growth eyes" come from? First, both John and Charles Wesley received new eyes as a gift within their 1738 "heartwarming experiences," in which the living God assured them of his acceptance and gave each the heart and vision of an apostle. J. Ernest Rattenbury, in *Wesley's Legacy to the World,* explains that the respective "conversion experiences" of Charles and John came within three days of each other, experiences in which each could now marvel "that I . . . should know, should feel my sins forgiven." In Charles' experience of justification, he was given a gift for hymn writing, and within two days he had written his first hymn! The night of May 24, 1738, John left the Aldersgate meeting, the scene of his "heart strangely warmed," walked to Charles' home, and entered exclaiming "I believe! I believe!" They sat at the piano and sang Charles' new hymn. Rattenbury explains that this first hymn "gets to the very heart of the evangelical experience, and its last verses . . . are strangely prophetic, not only of Charles Wesley's mission, but even more of John's" (Rattenbury, 1928, p. 65).

> And shall I slight my Father's love?
>   Or basely fear His gifts to own?
> Unmindful of His favours prove?
>   Shall I, the hallowed cross to shun,
> Refuse His righteousness to impart,
> By hiding it within my heart? . . .
>
> Outcasts of men, to you I call,
>   Harlots, and publicans, and thieves!
> He spreads His arms to embrace you all,
>   Sinners alone, His grace receives; . . .

He calls you now, invites you home;
Come, O my guilty brethren, come!

Rattenbury contends, "There can be no doubt that it was the luminous moment in the lives of both the Wesleys which changed their whole outlook on life and opened up to them a new world" (p. 67).

Second, Wesley's expanding wealth of data helped him "to lift up [his] eyes and see where the fields were white unto harvest." His expanding journal recorded important observations, interview data, historical analyses, reports from across the movement, theoretical conclusions, and so forth, and his frequent review of this data enabled him to systematize his insights, discern trends, and construct a body of practical strategic theory. The data, when he reviewed it, enabled him to see where responsiveness was likely.

As mentioned, Wesley's approach to receptivity flowed from his doctrine of prevenient grace, and became a key to discerning where God's prevenient grace was moving in people's hearts in a given season. He shifted his time and energy toward those thought to be responsive—the new urban working classes, mining peoples, Bristol, Cornwall, the North of England. In Ireland, Wesley found soldiers to be receptive; he preached in the barracks, and many soldiers became Methodist Christians. Indeed, many of the Irish people were open, so Wesley went to Ireland twenty times in forty-three years (Schmidt, 1972, p. 86).

Wesley knew, as we do today, that the receptivity principle is *not* a mathematically precise strategy for knowing in advance who will be responsive, or how responsive. Indeed, much theological mystery remains unexplained in our understanding of the gospel's communication and the varied responses of persons and peoples. But the receptivity principle is an informed way to "play the odds." For example, if a group decided to evangelize a ministry area randomly, as in serial door knocking, they would find 1 to 2 percent of the unchurched people responsive. Using "indicators" to identify likely receptive people, however, and investing the most time and energy with persons and groups who match the "indicators," they would find, say, 6 percent responsive, or 7 percent, or 8 or 9. At one point, Wesley declined an invitation to preach in a particular town, because "God will not suffer my little remaining strength to be spent on those who will not hear me, but in an honorable way" (*Journal,* July 6, 1754).

It remained for Donald McGavran to rediscover and amplify the receptivity principle in the twentieth century. His research concluded that

fluctuating receptivity is a most prominent aspect of human nature and society. . . . The receptivity or responsiveness of individuals waxes and wanes. No person is equally ready at all times to follow 'the Way' . . . . Peoples and societies also vary in responsiveness. Whole segments of mankind resist the Gospel for periods—often very long periods—and then ripen to the Good News . . . . Missions in Asia, Africa, and Latin America also abundantly illustrate the fact that societies ripen to the Gospel at different times . . . . Sudden ripenings, far from being unusual, are common . . . . One thing is clear—receptivity wanes as often as it waxes. Like the tide, it comes in and goes out. Unlike the tide, no one can guarantee when it goes out that it will soon come back again. (McGavran, 1980, pp. 245-48)

So McGavran concludes that reaching receptive people while they are receptive is, in each season, the most urgent priority in the church's mission. Furthermore, "An essential task is to discern receptivity and—when this is seen—to adjust methods, institutions, and personnel until the receptive are becoming Christians and reaching out to win their fellows to eternal life" (p. 265). McGavran's colleague Arthur Glasser underscores the importance of the principle and explains that

there is a time when God's Spirit is peculiarly active in the hearts of men. They become "ripe unto harvest." As a result, all evangelistic activity should be in response to an awareness of where God is at work. Down through the years, as a result of a great deal of "soil testing" and field research, we have found that wherever this empirical factor has been deliberately made determinative of strategy, God has abundantly confirmed with good harvests. Indeed we feel we have leaped over the inscrutable mystery that down through the years has provoked endless theological debate and ecclesiastical division, and have put strength where it furthers, not hinders, the ongoing of the Christian mission. In seeking to win those whom God has made winnable we have not unnaturally gained new insight into what it means to be co-laborers with God in the building of His Church. (from Conn. ed., 1976)

Theological Achievements

At one level, the principle of receptivity is unremarkable, representing common sense insights into human nature and common sense ways in which people cope with, and influence, one another. For instance, when a young man asks permission to use the family car, he asks his dad after the evening meal, since his dad is more amenable to suggestion after a good meal than before. Again, most any suitor senses that he must ask for his sweetheart's hand in marriage neither too soon nor too late. If he "pops the question" before she is ready, it can frighten or alienate her. If he waits too long, she may look for greener pastures. The principle has long been recognized in human affairs. In Shakespeare's *Julius Caesar*, Brutus recognized that

> There is a tide in the affairs of men,
> Which, taken at the flood, leads on to fortune;
> Omitted, all the voyage of their life
> Is bound in shallows and in miseries.

Lesser literatures in fields like "time management" and "salesmanship" emphasize, in quite human terms, the same principle. For instance, Merrill and Donna Douglass, in *Manage Your Time, Manage Your Work, Manage Yourself*, devote a chapter to managing sales time and suggest that "most salesmen would be better off if they dropped 10 to 20 percent of their present customers and concentrated on those customers with greater potential purchasing power" (p. 212). Using two criteria, (1) their *responsiveness*, and (2) their potential *value* as customers, the Douglasses counsel sales people to classify prospects or customers as "A" (top 10%), "B" (high 20%), "C" (middle 40%), "D" (a lower 20%), and "E" (a "least valuable" 10%). "Your best bet, then, is to call on the highest-value accounts or prospects first."

Most theologically educated Christians resist insights from apparently secular, materialistic, literatures. In truth, the insights from any secular literature should be selectively appropriated for the church's use, filtered through the church's ethic, and adapted in appropriate ways. For instance, Christians should not appraise some undiscipled people as "least valuable" and abandon these "clients." Christians are not called to write anyone off until the Hound of Heaven does! Church Growth has developed a careful and caring policy toward "resistant populations" that does *not* counsel abandoning such people, as we shall see, but such dissimilar schools of thought as Church Growth theory and Sales Psychology theory concur in perceiving that some people are more responsive to a particular product, service, truth claim, or movement than others, and practical wisdom takes that fact seriously.

Again, something within us resists the suggestion that some people are "more valuable" than others, for "God is no respecter of persons," but it cannot be denied that some people are "more valuable" to particular causes or objectives than others. Christian social advocates wisely extend more priority time and energy to influence, in Washington, D.C., the president's cabinet and Congress than they spend to influence a similar number of randomly selected people in, say, Uleta, Florida. And cross-culture missionaries have, through the centuries, wisely prioritized their witness to kings, tribal chiefs, opinion leaders, and people with many friends or relatives.

So at one level, the principle of receptivity reminds us of what people, intuitively, have always known. Yet, there are reasons for Glasser to report, "We feel we have leaped over the inscrutable mystery that down through the years has provoked endless theological debate and ecclesiastical division." Those reasons reside in such theological insights as the following.

First, receptivity theory helps us transcend Calvinism's conclusion that some people are "not elected" by God for salvation. To be sure, John Calvin was addressing a profound mystery, and it is possible to imagine how he reached his conclusion: The major premise of his whole theological system was the sovereignty of God. He also believed, and I think experienced, the grace of this sovereign God to be "irresistible." But he observed some people in Geneva resisting the preached offer of "irresistible grace." How do

you reconcile, logically, the sovereignty of God, the irresisti-
bility of grace, and the empirical fact of a resisting
population? You conclude that some people are not created
with the capacity to respond to grace.

Calvin's mistake, I think, is like photographing a group of
people and concluding that "they have always looked like that
and always will." He did not recognize that receptivity "waxes
and wanes" in persons and peoples. Wesley did. His field-
researched "longitudinal study" of many towns and peoples
of England enabled him to perceive fluctuations over time in
people's degree of responsiveness, that people who are
resistant now may be receptive later. Wesley seemed driven
by the hypothesis that *all* people are receptive some of the
time! McGavran and most other Church Growth people now
share Wesley's general reading of humanity.

Second, the insight that receptivity fluctuates provides us
with a new source of evangelistic urgency. Christians who are
no longer energized by the Edwardsean scene of unsaved
people dangling over Hell are sometimes energized by the
realization that receptive people are not so forever, that it is
urgent that we reach them while they are receptive, lest we
miss the day of their visitation and God's judgment be upon
us!

Third, receptivity theory awakens us to a widespread
problem in today's church—"closet predestinarianism"!
Though most Christians today would disavow the doctrine of
double predestination, many still behave in ways that reveal
their assumption that (because of appearance, religion,
culture, life-style, or political opinions) some people are
unreachable, beyond hope, or could never become *real*
Christians "like us"!

Fourth, receptivity theory helps us address the perennial
question of whether to commend the gospel to persons
influenced by some other major religious tradition, such as
Hinduism, Buddhism, Islam, or even Marxism. The implications of receptivity theory clearly point to two conclusions:
(1) If, say, a group of Moslems or Marxists are now "satisfied"
with their religion, it would be counterproductive in any case
to saturate that population with gospel witness; McGavran
counsels a "light presence" for the time being. (2) If a group

of people, regardless of their religious background or conditioning, are now dissatisfied with their religion and are open or receptive to something else, this is because prevenient grace is now active within and among them. There are no theologically valid reasons for withholding the gospel from a people whom the Lord of the Harvest is preparing.

Fifth, the principle helps in the contemporary restoration of "apostolic confidence." When Christians assume *they* are responsible for preparing, evangelizing, and converting people, most of them shrink from such an awesome responsibility—for which they feel neither prepared nor worthy. But when Christians see that *the Holy Spirit* prepares people, and empowers and leads us to them, that he makes his appeal through us, and that he is responsible for revelation and conversion, Christians then feel liberated to perform their role with God's mission.

Seed Planting

Granted that receptive people are the church's urgent opportunity in each season, what should be the church's policy toward resistant people who have no interest, at least for now, in becoming Christians? As suggested above, in contrast with "sales strategy," we are *not* to abandon such people or write them off. Rather, as Donald McGavran has advised:

Abandonment is not called for. Fields must be sown. Stony fields must be plowed before they are sown. No one should conclude that if receptivity is low, the Church should withdraw mission.

Correct policy is to occupy fields of low receptivity lightly. They will return receptive some day. They also have children of God living in them. Their populations are made up of men and women for whom Christ died. While they continue in their rebellious and resistant state, they should be given the opportunity to hear the gospel in as courteous a way as possible. But they should not be heavily occupied lest, fearing that they will be swamped by Christians, they become even more resistant.

They should not be bothered or badgered . . . Resistant lands should be held lightly.

While holding them lightly, Christian mission should perfect organizational arrangements so that when these lands turn responsive, missionary resources can be sent in quickly. (1980, p. 262)

While John Wesley's strategy, like McGavran's, stressed identifying the harvests, moving toward receptivity, and winning the winnable, Wesley also reserved some priority energy for the pre-evangelism of resistant people, even hostile people. Wesley's most conspicuous medium for this ministry was field preaching to *mobs!* His journal, particularly in the early years of the movement, is filled with firsthand accounts of his experiences preaching to "the many headed beast." Often hoodlums abused him, several times they hurt him, and occasionally he was in mortal danger.

But he acquired some knowledge of the unusual art of controlling mobs. He discovered that planting Methodist supporters in the midst of a crowd could have a tranquilizing effect on the crowd dynamics, so he "sprinkled" such crowds with his own people. He advised his preachers to "always look a mob in the face," and he characteristically spoke to detractors and potential abusers directly, and this sometimes reduced opposition:

I preached at seven . . . in old Aberdeen. A large number of people were all attention; but there were many rude, stupid creatures round about them who knew as little of reason as religion. I never saw such brutes in Scotland before. One of them threw a potato, which fell on my arm; I turned to them, and some were ashamed. (*Journal*, May 1, 1768)

And one night, in Canterbury in 1750, "A few turbulent people made a little noise, as I found it was the custom to do. Perceiving more of them were gathered the next night, I turned and spoke to them at large. They appeared to be not a little confounded and went away as quiet as lambs" (*Journal*, December 13, 1750). On another night that same year in Ireland, however, four men began ignoring Wesley's address and talking loudly to one another. Wesley reports, "I mildly reproved them, on which they rose up and went away, railing and blaspheming!" (*Journal*, March 29, 1750).

Speaking to mobs was an important component of Wesley's overall strategy for "the spread of true religion . . . in these three kingdoms." His ministry to resistant populations appears to have contributed to Methodism's contagion in several ways.

First, Wesley felt called to preach the gospel to all people, in season and out of season. This ministry was in obedience to God, and if any results came from a single witness to a resistant population, it was due to the Holy Spirit. So, in Kendall, "I once more 'cast' my 'bread upon the waters' and left the event to God" (*Journal*, April 11, 1768). Where necessary, Wesley also left to God the results of an unproductive long-term ministry of presence. Wesley reflects, in Dungiven, Ireland, that

in no other place in Ireland have more pains been taken by the most able of our preachers. And to how little purpose! Bands they have none; four and forty persons in society. The greater part of these heartless and cold. The audience in general dead as stones. However, we are to deliver our message; and let our Lord do as seemeth Him good. (*Journal*, April 20, 1769)

Second, preaching to mobs established the public credibility of Methodism as a movement that both cared and dared. Most people are not epistemologists who know how, logically, to evaluate competing truth claims. Most people judge as most believable those advocates who seem most to believe their message—as evidenced by sacrificing, paying a price, or taking risks for their beliefs. The common people of England were used to religious authorities who played it safe. Wesley, and many of his preachers, presented the people with an alternative and contagious model—embodied in men and women who endured the hardship of itineracy and took personal risks for the people they wanted to reach. This drama undoubtedly contributed to Methodism's image and its dynamic public appeal.

Third, Wesley seems to have returned to formerly resistant areas to "test the soils" and see whether the area was becoming more receptive. The mission dare not completely abandon a population, lest they turn receptive and Christian leaders not see the ripening harvest. As Wesley periodically revisited certain fields, he would note those where, over the years, resistance shifted to receptivity, or even to enthusiastic responsiveness.

In the evening I preached in a kind of square at Colne, to a multitude of people, all drinking in the Word. I scarcely ever saw a congregation wherein men, women, and children stood in such a posture; and this in the town wherein, thirty years ago, no Methodist could show his head. (*Journal*, April 30, 1776)

I rode to Birmingham. This had been long a dry, uncomfortable place; so I expected little good here. But I was happily disappointed. Such a congregation I never saw there before; not a scoffer, not a trifler, not an inattentive person (so far as I could discern) among them; and seldom have I known so deep, solemn a sense of the power, and presence, and love of God . . . . Will then God at length cause even this barren wilderness to blossom and bud as the rose? (*Journal*, October 20, 1749)

The last time I was here [Falmouth], about forty years ago, I was taken prisoner by an immense mob, gaping and roaring like lions. But how is the tide turned! High and low now lined the street, from one end of the town to the other, . . . gaping and staring as if the king were going by.

He was able to preach on that occasion in Falmouth, and "God moved wonderfully on the hearts of the people, who all seemed to know the day of their visitation" (*Journal*, August 17, 1789).

Fourth, Wesley saw the ministry to resistant people as an investment in, and one cause of, their later receptivity. By loving them and proclaiming to them now, one is planting the seeds that will germinate and flower in God's good time. This is the lesson of a well-known story in Wesley's life. Early in the movement Wesley journeyed to Epworth to preach to his own townspeople, only to discover that his father's successor as rector of Epworth had closed the church to Wesley. But someone spread the rumor that, at an announced time, Wesley would speak in the graveyard beside the church. A vast crowd assembled, and Wesley stood on his father's tombstone to project his voice and see the crowd, and many people were responsive. That night, Wesley wrote in his journal:

Oh, let none of you think his labor of love is lost because the fruit does not immediately appear! Nearly forty years did my father labour here, but he saw little fruit of all his labour. I took some pains among this people too, and my strength also seemed spent in vain; but now the fruit appeared. There were scarcely any in the town on whom either my father or I had taken any pains formerly but the seed, sown so long since, now sprang up, bringing forth repentence and remission of sins. (*Journal*, June 13, 1742)

In addition to the categories of receptive people and resistant people, Wesley identified "genteel" people "who profess religion," to whom he ministered, but as little as possible! He found them immunized against full salvation, and he worked among them sparingly because of their effect upon the spirit of ministers! Ministry to receptive people and to resistant people strengthens one's spirit and one's theology, but ministry to the genteel religious people has a subtly destructive effect upon the one who ministers. Both Wesley and Joseph Fletcher (Wesley's designated successor until Fletcher's death) experienced this phenomenon, and in one letter to Fletcher, Wesley confessed,

The conversing with them I have rarely found to be profitable to my soul. Rather, it has dampened my desires, and has cooled my resolutions: And I have commonly left them with a dry, dissipated spirit.
    And how can you expect it to be otherwise? For do we not naturally catch their spirit with whom we converse? . . . Certainly, then, if you converse much with such persons, you will return less a man than you were before. (*Works*, Vol. 12, pp. 161-62)

In our generation, in which the morale of the clergy is considered epidemically low, Mr. Wesley's insight has therapeutic implications. My own spot checks of clergy with low morale reveals that much of their time with people is spent with their church members or other genteel religious people, or in judicatory meetings and activities, with precious little time spent with either resistant pagans or receptive undiscipled people.

Thirteen "Indicators" of Receptivity

I served, in the late 1960s, two "inner belt" Methodist churches in Birmingham, England, with two colleagues,

Trevor Rowe and Gwen Bell. One day Trevor and I observed a map of our section of Birmingham, which was then populated by 150,000 persons—Anglos, West Indians, and Pakistanis, at least 90 percent unchurched. At least "2 percent of those unchurched people would be receptive to one of our churches if we befriended and invited them," I guessed. Trevor agreed, but added, "Among such a massive population, how do you identify them?" Today, we recommend the known "indicators of possible receptivity" for meeting that imposing challenge.

"Indicators" are the observable conditions or phenomena that frequently precede or accompany the increased responsiveness of people and the growth of the church. From several decades of research and reflection, it is possible to generate an unmanageably lengthy list. However, by combining some and thinking generically, we can delineate an even dozen, adding one. We do not use indicators in order to supplant a spiritual matter with secular technology, but rather as lenses to help us spot where the Spirit is preparing people and calling us to join him. When we pray to be led to prepared people, we find them or "run into" them, frequently by "coincidence"! Cease such praying, and the "coincidences" cease. (The first four indicators show how the principle of receptivity overlaps, in part, with the four mega-strategies of the next four chapters.)

1. Unchurched people who are linked, by *kinship or friendship networks,* to the church's active credible Christians are more receptive than other people. Undiscipled people tend to become potentially receptive, even emotionally involved, when someone in their social network becomes a genuine Christian. Typically, the church grows when it spreads to the friends, relatives, neighbors, and coworkers of its members, especially its new members and converts. Churches grow when they periodically survey their members and identify all the ministry area's undiscipled people who are linked to believers.

2. People are more receptive to outreach from *new groups and classes* than from long established groups and classes. Furthermore, a first generation church can attract some

people that an older congregation cannot. We are sure of at least two reasons: (a) Some people like to "get in on the ground floor." They are more interested in pursuing an agenda they helped create than an agenda someone else created that "I do not own." (b) New groups and churches do not experience, as much as older groups and churches, the conflict between the "pioneers" and the "homesteaders," with the homesteaders feeling outside the fellowship of those who "remember back when."

3. Churches grow as they identify *people with needs* that the church can minister to, either by (a) extending ministries already in place, or (b) building new ministries. To illustrate how ministries can be extended, in the years that Charles Allen pastored Grace Methodist Church in Atlanta, Georgia (1948–60), he extended the church's ministry to unchurched persons engaged to be married, removing all church policies (such as fees) that might be interpreted as "we don't really want you." In those twelve years, Allen married 1,113 couples. Every couple was visited in the week following the wedding, and 327 couples joined Grace Church from that one ministry. Allen's rationale for wedding-related outreach is deceptively simple: "You have an attachment to where you got married!"

Sometimes, launching a new ministry is required to meet needs. Leaders at Richland, Washington's Central United Protestant Church, noted many of the community's families experiencing siege and deterioration. They redirected the goal of their outreach from reaching individuals to reaching families. The church provided marriage enrichment, marriage encounter weekends, and parent effectiveness training for hundreds of unchurched couples in the city. Pastor Joe Harding reports that couples frequently make Christian commitments in a typical marriage encounter weekend. He also reports that the listening skills that parents learn in parent effectiveness training are the very skills that prepare many of them to do effective visitation evangelism.

4. Sometimes, a more *indigenous ministry* will reveal a people to be receptive. This principle of indigenous ministry explains more than might be apparent. It explains why John Wesley found England's working people receptive, the very

people the parish churches had found resistant. It explains what happened in a blue collar neighborhood where a Presbyterian church experienced so much membership decline and lack of response that the building was sold. An Assembly of God congregation bought the building and within a year it was full and facing building plans. Interviews with the Assembly's new members (from the neighborhood) revealed that the new pastor and congregation "understood us," "fit the neighborhood," "spoke our language," and "sang songs we like," whereas the former church, at least in their perceptions, had not.

5. *Populations in which any religion is growing* should be perceived as open and searching for something. Roy Shearer suggests this indication may be the only reasonably perfect one. Obviously, "Wherever we see a growing non-Christian religion, we can be sure the people in that place are potential receptors of the gospel" (Shearer, 1973, pp. 162-63). We observe this indicator not only in the growth of a traditional religion, like Islam, but also in the growth of ideologies, quasi-religions, and cults—such as communism, nationalism, or Jonestown. In every case, the religion is engaging people's felt needs, but Christians need not assume the religion is meeting their deep needs.

But what if the growing religion is a Christian church of your own, or another, denomination? The conventional ecumenical wisdom would counsel you to "stay out of their territory," but both Wesley and modern Church Growth people question whether static-free interchurch relations should be our first rule, to which all other rules are subordinate. Both conclude that the size of the harvest should determine how many laborers are needed to gather it. If another church enters a field larger than it can manage, that field needs more laborers! No one church can gather all of a significant harvest. Its style will be indigenous to some of the people, but not to others. Its ministries will meet the needs of some people, but not those of others. So, there are no compelling reasons for withholding from receptive people the option of discipleship through your church.

6. *People among whom any religion has experienced decline* tend to be receptive. For instance, with the partial eclipse of Shinto

in Japan and of Confucianism throughout much of Asia, many peoples have experienced a religious vacuum that will, sooner or later, be filled with something. As many people in China, Russia, and their satellites become disillusioned with the utopian promises of Marxism, those peoples will constitute receptive mission fields. In many nations and peoples, the inherited folk religions are being jeopardized by the forces of technology, urbanization, and secularization, and their people are open to an alternative faith. McGavran writes that, "Man is a believer by nature. If faith in old religion fades he becomes responsive to some new religion— of science, communism, or an updated version of his ancestral cult. He may deify a new leader, his secular civilization, a political party, or Man—but worship he will" (McGavran, 1970, p. 233).

As a variant of the same principle, individuals who have recently lost faith in anything—a religion, a philosophy, a lover, a drug, a pipe dream, a utopian promise, or in themselves—tend to look for something new upon which to norm and inform their lives. The missionary congregation should constantly be on the lookout for people who are "between idols."

7. *A people experiencing major culture change* tend to be very receptive. Culture change takes a number of forms, such as decline of traditional values, or changes in marriage and family patterns or values, or changes in kinship structures or patterns. A range of changes in a society's political system, from being conquered to being liberated, from oppression imposed to oppression removed, from revolution to nationalism, have all contributed to the receptivity of a people. Major economic changes, such as unemployment, underemployment, runaway inflation, mergers, acquisitions, crop failures, and plant closings have all shaken people's false securities and opened them to the gospel.

8. Various forms of *population mobility* induce receptivity. For instance, new settlements are strategic centers for planting new congregations. Peter Wagner reports that "areas of rapid urbanization almost invariably contain large segments of population receptive to the gospel" (Wagner, 1971, p. 112). McGavran reminds us that

every American pastor is well aware of the fact that new suburbs in which there are no churches whatever are an excellent field in which to plant congregations. And new arrivals in any community yield a much higher proportion of new Christians than old inhabitants. Newcomers are looking for community and are open to new decisions; but they must be purposely evangelized.

Travel sometimes turns people responsive. Soldiers in World War II who had seen the world came back to resistant tribal areas of Africa and sparked movements to the Christian faith. (1980, p. 249)

9. In most seasons, in most nations, *"the masses" are more responsive than "the classes."* Much evangelism has presupposed the opposite, that if you first win the people with education, wealth, culture, and influence, then Christianity will "trickle down" to the masses. But this approach has aborted thousands of possibilities for the spread of the gospel. Indeed, Toynbee demonstrated that a new religion is usually accepted first by the proletariat and later by the more privileged (cited in McGavran, 1980, p. 284). Wesley saw that the faith must necessarily spread first from those people with no power so that others might perceive it to be of the power of God. Bishop Pickett's extensive research and experience convinced him that "there is strong reason to believe that the surest way of multiplying conversions of higher caste Hindus is to increase the scale on which the transforming, enriching and uplifting grace of Christ is demonstrated in the Depressed Classes. And one certain way to arrest the movements of the higher castes to Christ is to turn away from the poor and the despised (Pickett, 1960, p. 95).

We can understand this factor more precisely through the lenses of missionary anthropologist and linguist, Eugene Nida. In *Message and Mission: The Communication of the Christian Faith,* Nida presents conclusions from research in many nations (including all nations in the Western Hemisphere) showing the existence of six classes (based on factors like wealth, influence, education, ancestry, and talent) in every society:

1. Upper upper   People of inherited wealth and prestige.
2. Lower upper   People of new wealth, the top professional and managerial people.

3. Upper middle   Most professional and managerial people.
4. Lower middle   White collar, educated.
5. Upper lower   Skilled workers, literate.
6. Lower lower   Unskilled workers, many unemployed, many nonliterate.

There are variations, from nation to nation, in the percentage of people in a given class. In Haiti, the great majority are lower lower class; in Uruguay, many are upper middle class. Furthermore, nations vary in the degree to which vertical mobility is possible: In the United States many people move "up"; in India few do; and Brazil's inflation has caused much downward mobility.

It can be argued that the United States has a middle middle class in addition to the other six, but granting such variations, the six classes are identifiable in each society. What is important here is that whenever a Protestant church has shown great sustained growth, it has grown from the lower middle class and especially from the upper lower class. Protestant Christianity has *not* been notably effective among the lower lower class. For example, eighteenth-century Methodism drew from the upper lower class (and some from the lower middle class) but not much from the poorest of the poor. This has long been recognized. Early in this century, British Methodist leader Hugh Price Hughes cited with agreement a still earlier recognition that "Wesley's itineraries were deliberately planned to bring him into direct contact neither with the aristocracy nor with the dependent or poverty-stricken poor, but with the industrious self-supporting workmen in town and country" (*see* Hughes' "Introduction" in Parker, n.d.). The early Methodists engaged in much ministry with the "dependent poor," and Wesley hoped many of them could be awakened, but little Methodist church growth took place among them.

Protestant history knows few exceptions. (India is one that comes to mind. Its caste system is based solely upon ancestry, with a number of "untouchables" who are literate, with leadership experience, and so forth. Protestant churches there have grown in a hundred or so of India's lowest castes.)

One reason may be that Protestant Christianity generally presupposes that people are literate enough to read the Bible, and that they are interested in following "left-brained" discourse and even lengthy arguments—presuppositions that may not fit large numbers of the lowest population strata.

Roman Catholicism and Pentecostal Christianity have demonstrated some ability to attract the lower lower classes. Reasons may include Catholicism's use of visual media (such as stained-glass windows) to tell the Story. Catholics also respect the capacity of oral tradition peoples for memorizing, and using memorization (such as the catechism) to teach them. In Pentecostalism, it could be that Pentecostal pageantry engages many of these people, and their more indigenous liturgy permits emotional expressions from ecstasy to catharsis.

Nida and McGavran show that when Protestant churches do grow, their very growth sows the seeds for their later stagnation. As people are discipled from the upper lower class, they gradually gain literacy, a new self-image, raised self-esteem, education, leadership experience, dignity as a people, hope for the future, raised aspirations, and so on. They experience "redemption and lift" (*see* McGavran, 1980, ch. 15), moving up the social scale to lower middle class or upper middle class. This phenomenon is a (widely unrecognized) key to Christianity's ministry of social reform. Indeed, probably more people have been liberated from disadvantage and oppressive conditions through discipleship than through social reform campaigns.

But (as usual) there is a trade-off: Discipled people become, indeed, different people—with vocabulary, values, habits, life-styles, and aspirations different from those remaining in the ranks they came from. They are now cut off from those ranks, a fact frequently felt more by those left behind than those who have advanced, and they no longer communicate naturally. At this point, the growth of the church plateaus—unless the denomination continues to start new work, including new congregations, with upper lower class peoples.

10. *People who are "like" the people already active* in a church, particularly its newer members, will be more receptive than

the surrounding population as a whole. Some churches systematically classify—in terms like age, culture, education, vocation, and class—the people they have received. They interview their new members to discover what was happening in their lives that made them receptive, the needs they felt at the time, the ministries, groups, experiences, and the truths that seemed to help, and so forth. Then they find many people like them and make those same ministries, groups, experiences, and truths available to them.

Some people, understandably, resist the idea of reaching out to "people like us." They want a church that proportionately represents all the peoples in the ministry area. Church Growth thought contributes some badly needed realism to this dilemma: (a) No church is equally effective in outreach to each group in its ministry area. A church is always more effective at attracting some types of people than others. (b) A church is already, demonstrably, effective at reaching the kind of people it is already reaching. That church is called to identify and reach as many people like them as possible, and in this way experience growth that is (comparatively) easy to come by. (c) As the church grows, it experiences an increase in the human resources and financial resources available for its whole mission, including resources for the staff, program, and volunteers necessary to reach *different* population groups.

11. *Personal dissatisfaction* with themselves and their lives opens many people to a gospel of grace and a second chance. Roy Shearer has observed that many receptive people are not able to satisfy their life needs and are open to something new that will (Shearer, 1973, p. 172). Through the ministry of a Lutheran church, a young man who had "tried everything in town to get in touch with my potential" found that his Creator knew him and had a purpose for his life. A teenager struggling with the power of temptation met his resurrected Lord in an Easter service. A twice estranged couple found the glue for an enduring reconciliation. An immigrant family found "support in our culture shock, and now this whole church is our tribe."

12. *Persons experiencing important life transitions* are more receptive than persons in stable periods of life. In every

season, many persons are experiencing some major change in their lives or social roles, and this tends to "unfreeze" their lives and makes change possible. The kinds of receptivity-increasing transitions that people experience include adolescence, going to college (or the armed forces), first job, getting married, first child, last child leaving home, menopause, mid-life crisis, retirement, loss of loved one, and other similar experiences. Additional receptivity-inducing transitions that many people experience include birth (or adoption) of a sibling, moving to a new community, getting fired, job advancement, separation, divorce, and second marriage. Notice that not all of these transitions are necessarily experienced as "crises." Nontraumatic transitions can still induce receptivity.

A church, in basing strategy upon this principle, can prepare cadres of its members for specific outreach ministry to persons undergoing such transitions. The gifts, interests, expertise, or backgrounds of laypersons would be "matched," in teams, to persons experiencing a particular transition. For instance, a team of two or three Christians with divorce in their backgrounds can be recruited to share the resources of grace and *koinonia* they discovered during their own painful transitions. Retired persons, who felt obsolete but have found new purpose in discipleship, can reach out to persons retiring from jobs, and so forth.

The church can build this ministry in two ways: (a) It can identify and organize a team of several laypersons for each of the transitions that are observed in the ministry area and for which the church has some strength for ministry. (b) The church can encourage the entire congregation to support a referral system. Under this system, members telephone the ministry's coordinator with data about persons in their neighborhoods experiencing divorce, retirement, or other transitions. The coordinator then relays the data to the leader of the appropriate outreach group. This comprehensive strategy can reach many receptive people and can use many Christians, equipped by their experiences, for outreach.

13. *Visitors to a church's worship service* are frequently receptive to that church—at least for a short period of time. Whether church leaders know it or not, visitors use a worship

service as a "shop window"—to observe and sample the church's goods, to determine how comfortable they are with the church's people, to detect what the church believes and lives for, to see whether they "like it," and to see whether the members notice, welcome, and want them. Effective pastors modify their liturgy to make it possible for visitors to follow and understand, and they schedule times for people to notice and greet one another.

Regarding visitors, Herb Miller, a Disciples of Christ executive in the United States, tells churches they have to develop clear answers to six questions: Does the church (a) want, (b) seek, (c) invite, (d) welcome, (e) involve, and (f) nurture company? These six questions are relevant to the church's Sunday visitors, and to the fact that they are frequently receptive—for a short period of time. Miller reports that when someone from the church responds with a brief, get-acquainted visit within thirty-six hours, about 85 percent of first-time visitors return. When the visit is within seventy-two hours, about 60 percent return. Those percentages apply to visits by laypeople. When the visit is made by a pastor, the percentages are cut in half! Miller reports that "pastors are not as effective on calls because people are looking for a sign of friendliness. People are smart enough to know that the pastor is on the payroll. He is supposed to do things like visit" (*United Methodist Reporter*, September 20, 1985).

A Challenge to the Theory

Sometimes a new church will win some receptive people in a community and show early growth to, say, sixty or eighty members—and then grow no more. Sometimes a new denomination will be planted in a nation or region, will find some receptive people and grow to, say, three or four dozen congregations, and two thousand to three thousand members, and will then prematurely level off.

These two versions of the same phenomenon have long perplexed Christian leaders and suggest, at least, that getting a church started and growing is not the same as keeping it growing. Churches share this mystery with other organizations. As this is written Stephen Jobs, Apple Computer's entrepreneurial cofounder, has resigned as chairman of Apple's board following the removal of most of his power several months ago. The very factors that made him an early asset appear to have been a liability to the organization's long-term health.

Reflecting on the life history of such churches and organizations, several insights may explain the stunted growth of churches in some situations:

1. The skills necessary to start something well are not the same skills needed to keep something growing. This was Apple's discovery, and many churches discover that the excellent catalytic church planter who was the right person to start the church is not the same person needed to keep it growing.
2. A major shift in leadership style is necessary to maintain growth. In situations where the entrepreneur or founding pastor maintains control and is unwilling or unable to include others in planning, to delegate responsibilities, and so forth, the organization's strength and achievements plateau. In churches where the "shepherd" is unable to acquire the skills of a "rancher," the church levels off to the number of members and groups that one shepherd can control.
3. Some leaders would rather control all the pieces of a small pie than allow a bigger pie to cook.
4. When a leveling off occurs, for whatever reasons, many people and leaders get used to it, come to regard that size as "natural," and resist the thought of growing larger or stronger or achieving more. "Our church is the right size now!"

I have long guessed that the type of person who first joins an organization, or a church, influences its potential for further development. For instance, the members of an average department of a college faculty will usually find "reasons" for not inviting a superior colleague to join their department. Again, some people join an organization and then work industriously to run their agenda over the organization's agenda; when such persons are not "exorcised" the organization proceeds to achieve neither the new agenda nor the old. Again, we have all seen how quickly some people form into cliques and unwittingly discourage or alienate prospective members. We also know that the human relations skills of the first members can influence how well the church proceeds and how well it attracts other persons into the fellowship.

Recently, the behavioral science literatures that help explain why any cause, movement, idea, or technology spreads in a society (*see* Rogers, 1983, chs. 7 and 8) have helped us see that there are two types of receptive people who, early, join a new church, or avail themselves of a new service, or use a new technology. This is important because the "innovation's" future "diffusion rate" depends partly on which of these two types first becomes involved. Everett M. Rogers, summarizing the insights to date in *Diffusion of Innovations,* lists five categories of "adopters" (based on when, during an innovation's spread, they adopt), and explains their basic characteristics: innovators; early adopters; early majority; late majority; and laggards. Rogers' discussion of the differences between "innovators" and "early adopters" has great implications for our present discussion.

The "early adopter" types are integrated into the community and have influence with many other people. They are respected, and looked up to, as opinion leaders and role models. When they adopt an innovation, they influence many other people to adopt it. Indeed, most people in a community characteristically check with, or ask for counsel from, these opinion leaders before they seriously consider adopting. When a movement begins with opinion leaders, its chances of diffusion throughout much of the community are excellent.

The "innovators," however, are often venturesome mavericks who are known to be quick to pursue almost any new idea. Their focus is more outside than inside the social system, and they are not greatly respected, trusted, or looked to for leadership from other groups in the community. Some of them are perceived as deviant.

We can guess that many churches that first grew, but quickly plateaued, first attracted and won some innovators, but not many opinion leaders. Since most of the visible charter members were not influential with others in the community, the growth peaked early and the church experienced relative isolation.

A strategically wise church planter would identify the community's opinion leaders, find some of them who are receptive, and disciple them before the new church is "chartered." The new church will then have the social credibility and social bridges necessary for sustained growth. A church seen to be composed of "mavericks" will not have that credibility and network.

There may be other reasons to qualify or bend the principle of receptivity, but we neglect its importance to the peril of many responsive people. McGavran reminds us that "opportunity blazes today, but it may be a brief blaze. Certainly conditions which create the opportunity—as far as human wisdom can discern—are transient conditions. We have today. Let us move forward" (1959, p. 9).

C H A P T E R   4

Reaching Out Across Social Networks

The discoveries of Church Growth research have revolutionized the way future Christians will spread the faith. While evangelicals already possess an inherited collection of assumptions, lore, approaches, and methods that "ought" to work, Church Growth scholars know that many approaches and methods that "ought" to produce fruits do *not* and some methods fail in places where the correct approach would identify and gather a harvest. Using the research methods of behavioral science—observation, questionnaires, historical analysis, and (especially) interviews—Church Growth researchers have separated fact from fiction, have invalidated many entrenched counter-productive myths, and have demonstrated the known ways churches advance.

For instance, Christians widely assume that Christian faith usually spreads impersonally (and instantly). The assumption is reflected in the methods that many sincere Christians use, from pamphlet distribution to radio and television broadcasting, to approaches to witnessing that primarily vocalize a rehearsed theological formula. The assumption is reflected in the nearly universal model of witnessing present in most Christian minds: that people *usually* become Christians when a Christian stranger, say, on a flight from Newark to Richmond, witnesses impromptu to a seatmate and, in one transaction, welcomes a new convert. In fact, it almost *never* happens that way! When such an unusual event does occur, the story spreads like a prairie fire, makes the cover of *Guideposts,* and Gospel Films produces another winner that plays twenty thousand Sunday evening services. Stories of the unusual reinforce the myth that they are the usual—or ought to be.

How the Faith Spreads

The Christian faith usually spreads through interpersonal influence (and is usually acquired in "stages," spread over weeks or months, or even years). In other words, the Christian faith usually spreads across the social networks of active credible Christians, especially new Christians. This was the first principle discovered by the earliest Church Growth research.

The generic version of this principle has been demonstrated in the extensive behavioral science writings on the diffusion of innovations, which asks, *how* new ideas, services, movements, and technologies spread in a society. Although a few people ("innovators" and "opinion leaders") discover and adopt new ideas, products, or technology, most people do not. Many people may, initially, know of a new possibility from a media message, but they adopt it only after the possibility has been made credible and recommended by a trusted opinion leader, or a peer, from within their "communication network" (*see* Rogers, 1983, ch. 8).

In Church Growth research, this principle was first seen operating in the movements of some of India's depressed classes into the Christian faith. Bishop J. Wascom Pickett's landmark *Christian Mass Movements in India* reported the case of Ditt, a dark, lame little man of the untouchable Chuhra caste of the 1870s. Upon his conversion at a mission station, Ditt—against the advice of the missionaries—immediately returned to his village, people, and trade, and experienced a period of ostracism. But he persevered and loved his people, and Pickett writes that

three months after his baptism he reappeared in Sailkot and presented his wife, his daughter, and two neighbors as candidates for baptism. He had taught them what he knew; they professed their faith and their purpose to follow Christ and had walked thirty miles to be baptized. After examining them, instructing them and praying with them, Mr. Martin administered the rite, whereupon they immediately started back to their village. Six months later Ditt brought four other men who were also adjudged ready for baptism. The missionaries were by now convinced that a work of God was in progress in Ditt's village. Ditt's humble occupation of buying and selling hides took him to many villages. Wherever he went he told his fellow Chuhras of Christ. Many abused him, but an increasing number heard him patiently, and before long groups here and there began to follow his lead. In the eleventh year after Ditt's conversion more than five hundred Chuhras were received into the Church. By 1900, more than half of these lowly people . . . had been converted, and by 1915 all but a few hundred members of the caste professed the Christian faith. (Pickett, 1933, pp. 43-45)

Pickett's account dramatizes the principle that Christianity spreads most contagiously along the social networks of credible Christians. (It also illustrates another principle, that the faith spreads more readily within a social unit than across social units.)

Donald McGavran "lit [his] candle at Pickett's fire" and used Pickett's discovery as a hypothesis for wider testing. Through twenty years of researching growing and non-growing churches in many tongues and cultures of Asia, Africa, and Latin America, McGavran demonstrated that Pickett's discovery is universal. In every land and tribe and tongue and culture in which the faith has spread, the social networks composed of the relatives and friends of believers have provided the bridges of God (McGavran, 1955). Faith is not usually spread by the mass media or by strangers, but by persons who are known and trusted by their hearers. The social networks of believers provide opportunity for a "web movement" of the Christian faith.

There are exceptions to this rule that fit the evangelical "myth," but some of the "exceptions," upon examination, prove the rule. For instance, interviews with some apparently instant converts reveal they had already experienced some stages of movement toward faith, however unapparent this was to others. Typically, they report disillusionment with some "idol," or a struggle for some unmet need, or a period of wondering and asking questions, or a period of observing the faces and lives of Christians. The evangelizer engaged them at a receptive period in their life history, gathering the harvest that was prepared but not obvious. In many cases where a person is won by a "stranger," the person *first* came to regard this Christian stranger as a trustworthy friend. As in many areas of life, many examined "exceptions" prove the rule.

Actually, several types of networks are involved in the spread of Christian faith. Sometimes *neighborhood networks* are potent. Frazier Memorial United Methodist Church in Montgomery, Alabama, has received more than one hundred families from "Arrowhead," a movement launched when one of the neighborhood's first four families joined Frazier and began inviting other new families. Sometimes *collegial networks* are potent, as one church in a city reaches many medical people, while another reaches teachers and their families.

More often, the potent contagious bridges are along *kinship networks* or *friendship networks*. These two types of networks vary in their influence. In Mexico, kinship bridges are responsible for a large majority of new converts. In Anglo populations of the United States, friendship networks are most potent. Lyle Schaller's research shows that two-thirds to three-quarters of all new church members in the United States respond because of someone in their kinship or friendship networks. In fast growing churches, the range is two-thirds to seven-eighths, and in very rapidly growing churches these two factors (especially friendship) account for more than 90 percent of new members (Schaller, September 3, 1975).

Of course, when any population of Christians is surveyed, some people say that a person was not their major bridge into the faith. In Win Arn's surveys for the Institute of American Church Growth, some 10 to 25 percent report the number-one cause of their joining as some factor other than a friend or relative (1982, p. 43). Occasionally the number attracted by other factors is somewhat larger. In 1983, some eight thousand Jewish converts responded to the question, What initially attracted you to the gospel, and what one agent most helped you to find the Lord? The *Jews for Jesus Newsletter* (1984, p. 4) published the results:

Initial Attraction to the Gospel

A person	47%
Search for truth	11%
Bible	8%
Book or other literature	8%
Supernatural intervention	6%
Group of believers	5%
Conviction/Holy Spirit	4%
Life crisis	3%
Radio/TV/Movies	2%
Curiosity	2%
Afterlife/Fear	1%
Ideals/World conditions	1%
No answer	4%

Of the 47 percent who reported "a person" as their bridge, 62 percent of these reported that the person was a friend or family member. This study, of the many similar studies of different Christian populations, shows perhaps the lowest percentage of conversions owing primarily to relational human bridges. Yet, even in this atypical ethnic population, social networks of Christians are far more potent than any other single factor in evangelism, and interviews would reveal that a strong trust of one or more Christians was an indispensable factor in evangelization, even if not recalled as the one most crucial factor.

From all such research, we see additional ways in which some traditional approaches to evangelism that "ought" to be prolific are not. The devotees of Bible distribution crusades cannot feel justified by research data, nor can TV evangelism, which is so far the least cost-effective medium for evangelism yet invented through human ingenuity. Since viewers exercise "selective exposure," those who view religious television are, overwhelmingly, those who already believe. Nonbelievers watch other channels. In any subject area, most people do not attend to messages that differ from what they already believe and value. The institutions devoted to revivals, preaching crusades, and so forth are also advised from research data to lift up their eyes and see what methods and approaches the Lord of the Harvest is (and is not) blessing to the building of his church. Special meetings that amplify the church's ongoing outreach continue to be productive, but special meetings held instead of the church's ongoing interpersonal outreach are achieving little.

Toward Social Network Strategy

If the social networks of Christians are the bridges of God, and if this is a supreme principle of informed Church Growth practice, *how* does one apply the principle to develop strategies? Explaining the principle is one thing, but using it to "make disciples" is another.

A Mennonite church in Japan employs the following strategy: They tutor, one on one, new members following conversion. Over three months, the trainer and convert (1) compile all the names of persons in the new convert's active social network. The trainer, near the end of the tutoring, (2) asks the convert to underline all the names of persons thought *not* to be active disciples through any congregation. The trainer (3) asks, Which of these (underlined) people do you have some influence with? Those names are circled, and the trainer and convert together reach out to each of those persons. As some of those persons are attracted and then admitted into discipleship, the strategy is repeated (McGavran and Hunter, 1980, pp. 35-36). Most churches could develop and execute a similar strategy, adapted to fit their culture and situation.

In a Church Growth manual written for congregations bent on finding the way forward, this writer offered strategic guidelines that have helped congregations. These guidelines are:

1. Secure the names of all undiscipled persons within the social webs of your active credible Christians. Have some member of your evangelism committee visit, with each active member, the undiscipled persons he or she has listed.

2. As you win some of those target persons, secure the names of *their* undiscipled relatives and friends. Have an evangelism committee member visit, with them, those people to be reached, etc.

3. Survey each member *each season* to get the names of new undiscipled prospects. This will continually reveal a fertile harvest field for your church—undiscipled persons who are already linked to one or more persons in your congregation.

4. As you reach out do *not* in every case attempt to gather Christ's prepared harvest in just one visit or conversation. Be prepared to visit with persons about the possibility a half-dozen or more times, to help them work through what their response to the invitation might be.

5. As some of your people begin serving as new bridges for others, *reinforce* this action through appropriate public *recognition*. For instance when you receive new members into the church, invite members who served as bridges for them to stand with them, and pray thanksgiving both for new disciples and their human bridges.

Recognition, appropriately conferred, may be the most neglected and the most cost-effective continuing strategy available in most churches today. Leaders completely control whom they publicly thank. It costs nothing except time—and precious little of that when well managed. Besides, our people have the impression that what gets recognition is most important in the organization and that which is not recognized is comparatively unimportant. So recognize your faith-bridge people. As the importance of their outreach is perceived, as their ministry is modeled for others, as their stories get around, and as the people meet their converts, their tribe will increase! (Hunter, 1980. [From pp. 20-21. © 1980 by Discipleship Resources, P. O. Box 840, Nashville, TN 37202. Used by permission.] Fifth point added)

Win and Charles Arn, in *The Master's Plan for Making Disciples,* base an entire approach to evangelism on this one principle. They see the principle modeled in the New Testament *oikos*—the extended "household" of family and friends that characterized an early Christian's sphere of intimates and to whom the faith was likely to spread.

The Arns declare that "webs of *common kinship* (the larger family), *common friendship* (friends and neighbors) and *common associates* (special interests, work relationships, and recreation) are still the paths most people follow in becoming Christians today." With variation by region, culture, and class, 75 percent to 90 percent report a friend or relative as the one factor most responsible for their joining (p. 43).

Many churches have experienced renaissance through using "the Master's Plan." In one case, the Reverend Brad

Dinsmore moved to the Lake Magdalen United Methodist Church in Tampa, Florida. He devoured *The Master's Plan,* had it studied in every class and group in the church, featured the film *For the Love of Pete,* and led Master's Plan workshops for other churches. In the last several years Lake Magdalen Church has experienced unprecedented growth and now is a Florida Methodism leader in net growth and new Christians received.

Sometimes, however, outreach across the existing social networks of our people is not a sufficiently potent strategy, for two reasons. First, many persons in greatest need of the church's ministry have smaller social networks than other people, and are less likely to be within a network that includes outreaching Christians. Second, after years of church involvement, many social networks of our people are largely confined to the church. These people do not know many undiscipled persons in their community, and may therefore assume there aren't many. In such cases, leaders need to expand the church's social networks by arousing the consciousness of members to the existence of undiscipled persons.

For example, at First United Methodist Church of Poplar Bluff, Missouri, the Reverend James Kennedy recently began asking participants of the meetings of his administrative board and council of ministries for the names of undiscipled people in the town. Such exercises generated no more than sixteen names, and sometimes as few as three. His people perceived no significant mission field in their "Christian" town of twenty-five thousand persons. Not long after, a small church committee worked through the entire Poplar Bluff telephone book, crossing through all the businesses and all names known to be connected to their church or any other, leaving some seventeen thousand possibly unchurched persons. They recruited seventeen members to telephone one hundred family units each and identified about twelve thousand unchurched people in Poplar Bluff—far more than any of the leaders had guessed were out there!

In spring of 1985, they sent brochures to each of these twelve thousand persons inviting them to church on Easter

Sunday. Several hundred came, and the leaders and members met as many as possible. They set up booths, with coffee and doughnuts, to welcome and meet singles, teenagers, "keen-agers" (senior citizens), and others. They launched a Wednes-day night emphasis, with options from seminars like "death and dying" to activities like "aerobics." They started new Wednesday night classes every six weeks, mailing invitations to the same population and supplementing the mailing with telephone calls and personal invitations. Through these Wednesday night "ports of entry," they have averaged twelve to fifteen visiting families with each effort (who are then visited in their homes within thirty-six hours) and have received at least one family a Sunday into church member-ship.

The church's whole approach to visitors has become much more calculated. "Welcome" signs have been posted at every entry, and each sign adds "This is the entry to . . . " Multiple greeters stand at each entrance, and a greeter walks with new persons to their destinations. The church has modified the worship service in ways that enable folks who are not "church broke" to know what to do, to follow the service, and to make sense of it.

An outreach group is calling on as many of the twelve thousand as possible who have not responded to the mailings. Kennedy reports that they have found and worked with two categories of unchurched people: (1) The *Unassuming*—who are surprised "that anyone would be interested in me." These people "bloom" when they perceive the church's interest in them is genuine and are visited a few times. (2) The *Arrogant*—who declare they can "make it on my own." They are "tougher" than the first group, but the church has so far been able to involve a group of them in a discussion class.

Human Relations in Faith's Spread

So there are ways to build new social bridges to unchurched people as well as reach across existing bridges, yet most Christians (including self-designated evangelicals) do not share their faith—despite reading books, attending workshops, and discussing evangelism. Many Christians confess they would like to do evangelistic ministry—but "not now," or "I still don't know how," or "I'm just not the type."

Several years ago this writer began interviewing laypersons (and pastors) who were already interested enough to attend an evangelism seminar but were not yet engaging in evangelism. The interviews revealed that, in regard to doing evangelism, most of them harbored more hang-ups than the city art gallery! What was the source of this resistance to the Great Commission? Gradually I came to realize that most Christians are immobilized by a stereotype of evangelists. Specifically, I identified four issues upon which most Christians flounder: (1) The types of persons who do evangelism, (2) the feelings involved within non-Christians, (3) the things evangelizers say, and (4) the things evangelizers do.

Undoubtably there are other issues, for the Evil One has strewn this path with many difficulties. I became confident of only those four, but what they enabled me to see astonished me as I pursued answers through more interviews. My research revealed the nature of the stereotype—extreme and unfair when reflected on, but nevertheless a stereotype almost universal among Christians, and incapacitating:

1. When reluctant evangelical Christians are asked to describe, by giving adjectives, their "image" of the type of person who most does evangelism, a clear caricature emerges. The following adjectives typically surface: aggressive, pushy, dogmatic, narrow-minded, hypocritical, overbearing, judgmental, fanatic, boastful, manipulative, ignorant, silver-tongued, moralistic, bombastic, arrogant, naive, square, emotional, critical, insensitive, imposing, doctrinaire, close-minded. People also mention some neutral adjectives, like bold, well-dressed, self-assured, outgoing, extravert; and they offer occasional positive adjectives, like authoritative, good at speaking, scholarly, risk taking, optimistic. More than 90 percent of the adjectives however are negative and alienating. That is the dominant image of the "type of people who go in for 'evangelism.'"

The problem is obvious. Our people do not identify with that image—though some believe they "ought" to want to. Upon reflection, everyone acknowledges the image to be an unfair stereotype. Subconsciously though, the image paralyzes many Christian souls and partly explains why Christians refrain from serving as ambassadors for Christ.

2. When Christians are asked what *feelings* they think the receivers of stereotypical evangelism experience, the "feeling words" most often generated are guilty, fearful-afraid-anxious, condemned-damned, inadequate, angry-hostile. Other frequent feeling words include inferior, uncomfortable, unworthy, intimidated, ignorant-dumb, worthless, cornered-trapped, pressured, turned off.

3. What do stereotypical evangelists *say?* The message of the stereotype is authoritarian, that is, a rehearsed authoritarian presentation that claims to be the only way to see things. Most Christians refrain from "evangelism" because they do not know how to communicate in those ways, and do not desire to!

4. What are stereotypical evangelists thought to *do?* The widely imaged behavior pattern pictures a monologue in which the evangelist is in control, is not genuinely interested in, or open to, the other person, gives the other no credit for knowing, believing, or having experienced anything worthwhile, and then demands a premature response. Upon examination, a large majority of these people have never, even once, been personally subjected to such "evangelism," but they all know, or know of, persons who have been!

The Church Growth scholar, acknowledging the widespread image of how evangelism alledgedly takes place, asks, How does it *really* take place? What kind of people *really* help others find their way into the faith and church? How do they make people feel? What messages do they communicate that help make a difference? What behaviors do they engage in that are influential?

For the past several years, when leading Church Growth

seminars in many denominations across the United States, and in Canada, Mexico, England, Japan, and South Africa, I have devoted one session simply to gathering data, which is then analyzed for the benefit of the seminar's participants. They are first instructed to write the name of the one person most responsible for their involvement with Christ and his church. If several names come to mind, they identify the most recent, or the person they most vividly recall. Then they respond to four questions: (1) What was this person like for you? Write the adjective that best describes this significant other in your life. (2) How did they make you feel, perhaps about yourself? Write a feeling word. (3) What, that you can recall more or less verbatim, did they say that helped make a difference? Write a message statement. (4) What did the person do that helped make a difference? Write a behavior. We spend the remainder of the session making a representative list of the responses to each of the four questions and we compare each list to the stereotype described above, though in the exercise we describe the stereotype last, without having referred to it earlier. When the two lists are posted, the insights are remarkable.

When Christians report the chief characteristic of their human bridge into discipleship, the two most cited adjectives are "caring" and "loving." Other adjectives are somewhat synonymous: encouraging, concerned, accepting, understanding, supporting, warm, affirming, sensitive, kind, and so on. Others report admirable or inspiring traits, like committed, believable, credible, patient, happy, fulfilled, honest, alive, friendly, humble, consistent, reasonable, authentic, stable, Christlike, positive, reliable, faithful.

Surprisingly, no one trait predominates. Different personalities with different needs respond to a wide variety of traits in other persons. Considering all the adjectives, there is always less than a 5 percent overlap between this list and the adjectives describing the stereotypical evangelist. A few adjectives reflecting the stereotype do surface, like persistent, confident, aggressive, winsome, persuasive, but the more extreme adjectives of the stereotype *never* surface in this data, and about half of all training groups generate no adjectives that overlap with the stereotype. This contrast between myth and reality is remarkably consistent in each of the several countries where I have led this exercise, and is consistent in various denominational groups from Church of God and Southern Baptist to Presbyterian and Christian Church, and the degree of contrast continues with the other three lists.

The feelings exemplified by persons asked to describe their idea of the typical evangelist, cited above, are probably the greatest single inner barrier to evangelism today. Most caring Christians have no interest in making people feel "that way"! The great news from this research is that those feelings are *not* the feelings that Christians report from the relationship with their human bridge. Indeed, it would be hard to imagine any greater contrast between myth and fact. In general, evangelized Christians report feeling more secure rather than less, better about themselves rather than worse, and less pressured rather than more. To be sure, people sometimes report being confronted or challenged, but they were free to respond, their rights were not encroached on, they did not feel trapped. The "feeling words" people often repeat are: accepted, important-special, loved, wanted-needed. Other typical feeling words include valued, affirmed, confident, worthwhile, supported, comfortable, included, free-liberated, having self-respect.

Whatever else evangelism is, so it is widely held, it is proclamation. To evangelize is to proclaim the glad tidings. Evangelism is the transmission of a message with accuracy, decision, and recall. The research presented here, however, paints a somewhat different picture. About half of all evangelical Christians have difficulty recalling *anything* their human bridge said that made the difference. Undoubtedly, the gospel was communicated to these people, that is, they comprehended its meaning from a number of persons, sources, and experiences, but their bridge person was not basically "proclaiming." Much more is involved in the ministry of evangelism than vocalizing a message, because people are much more than "souls with ears." Indeed, when Christians do remember conversations that made a great difference, the evangelist was doing about 80 percent listening and 20 percent talking. Furthermore, many people report "overhearing" a significant message.

Nevertheless, effective evangelism frequently involves saying something of the faith to another person. So, what do effective evangelists say? The sheer variety of remembered messages that made a difference is vast, and the examples that follow are random examples. Some messages, as one would expect, are theological affirmations: "Only God is foundation." "You are a child of God, created in his image." "God accepts you and loves you just as you are." "God has given you unique gifts." "A Christian does not have to be weird!" "Jesus died for you." "Christ can change your life." "God has a claim on your life." "Jesus can make something of your life." "God has a plan for your life." "No one is worthy, it is grace." As one can infer, the significant message is frequently as much about the recipient as about God or Christ.

Sometimes the message's main focus is the person being addressed. The data contributes no pattern, but one group generated this fairly typical list: "What have you done!" "Get involved." "In Christ you are somebody." "You can do it!" "There is a place for you." "There is a purpose for you." "Something good is going to happen to you." "You have a light, shine it." "You can be a part of God's family." "You are worth much more than you feel." "It matters to God what you do."

Sometimes the message reflects a relationship between messenger and recipient, or the messenger's perception of, or hopes for, the recipient. Random examples include: "You have a need for Christ." "We want you a lot." "I am concerned about your salvation." "I accept you as you are." "I am all for you." "You really are mixed up, aren't you?" "I believe this about you . . . "

Sometimes, but not as often as the stereotype would suggest, the evangelist will share his or her own relevant testimony, and more often a nugget than an autobiography: "It sure made all the difference in my life." "What I am and have, you can become." "I was just as anxious and down on myself as you are."

Sometimes the message is a powerful suggestion, or a probing question, that the person cannot shake off and thinks about again and again: "Who do you ultimately trust,

God or money?" "How long do you intend to ignore God's claim on your life?" "What is success, really?" "He is not against you, he is for you." Sometimes, the message is an open-ended question to which witness and respondent struggle for an answer together: "What do you think about . . . " "Should we . . . " "Where and how do we find God's will?" "How do you know when you've got it made?" "Describe the person you yearn to be."

The behaviors and actions that make a difference are also related to the person's need, struggle, or point of openness. For that reason, what Christians do that makes a difference is exceedingly varied: "She was there when I needed her." "She listened to me when I needed to talk it out." "He expressed concern for what was happening to me." "He shoveled the snow from my front walk." "He asked me to help in their ministry to blind people." "She invited me to play basketball." "They invited me to their home, as well as to church." "He gave me a Bible." "He loaned me a book, and we discussed it." "They didn't run away from my handicap." "He accepted me as I was." "She took me to lunch." "She encouraged me when I was down." "He helped me laugh again."

The data suggest several additional conclusions for informing effective evangelism ministry:

1. Effective faith-sharing is more relational than verbal.
2. The evangelist does much more listening than talking.
3. The evangelist vocalizes suggestions more than propositions.
4. Christianity is more caught than taught.
5. Conversion is almost never instant, but takes some weeks or months from insemination to new birth.
6. The occasions for evangelistic conversation usually arise situationally. The message is seldom a rehearsed theological formula out of a book or a packaged evangelistic program. It is usually specific, tailored to the recipient's felt need, point of openness, searching, or pain, and presents the facet of the gospel that is most immediately relevant.

7. In evangelism, the credibility, sensitivity, and skills of
    the communicator's human relations matter a great
    deal.

From established Church Growth research, we have
learned that the gospel spreads along the social networks of
living Christians. Now, we are beginning to learn *how* it
spreads—through effective human relations. This is fact.
What is false is that stereotype of the kinds of people who
evangelize, how they make people feel, what they do, what
they say. Most Christians are "not that type" and do not want
to be. They resist the possibility of saying "those things,"
doing "those things," and making people feel "that way." The
good news from research is that "that kind" of evangelism is
not what is taking place in the world, or at least is not the kind
that is producing new disciples in churches. There is no
evidence of any great reproductive work of *that* kind of
evangelism in our churches. Christians consistently relay
from their experiences a different picture.

The good news is that the people of God are far more
prepared and equipped to evangelize than we have assumed.
What is more, effective evangelism is not alien to our people,
their styles, their sensitivities, or their abilities. Indeed, the
kinds of people who best spread the faith are the kinds of
people our people already are, or would love to become.
Effective evangelists help people to feel in ways that are
congruent with our people's good will. Effective evangelists
say the kinds of things our people can say. They do the kinds
of things our people can do. This generation will see a vast
sleeping army awakened, prepared and equipped, at a time
when the church faces unprecedented opportunity in an
increasingly receptive world.

This "relational bridges" approach to effective evangelism
is widely observed where Christianity is an expanding
movement. Yet, even so great a strategist as Wesley did not
perceive this principle with the clarity and force it deserves,
and he did not emphasize it often in his advice to Methodists.
His journal and early Methodist history contain the data that
could lead an inductive mind to grasp it as a major principle,
but this one partly escaped his mental grasp.

Nevertheless, the principle partly explains the contagious expansion of eighteenth-century Methodism. Grace Murray was the bridge for her first husband's entry into faith, and she became the bridge for many people in northeastern England. Charles Wesley was the bridge for a large number of persons, including George Whitefield. John Wesley observes the principle in action from time to time, as when a Mr. G. "had lately contracted an acquaintance with Mr. R.," and met the wife of Mr. R., who persuaded him to read Mr. Wesley's "Earnest Appeal," which convinced him of reality in religion (*Journal*, January 6, 1748). Earlier, Wesley records that "I spent an hour with Mary Cheesebrook, a strange monument to the mercy of God. About six years ago, she was without God in the world, being a kept mistress. An acquaintance brought her one evening to the chapel in West Street, where God gave her a new heart" (*Journal*, November 22, 1747). The Methodist movement achieved a new credibility in Epworth when one man testified to his peers that "they have converted my wife. Till she went among them, she had such a tongue! And now she is quiet as a lamb." Apparently the town's men became keen about their wives getting that kind of religion! Wesley's journal is filled with allusions to the influence of parents, or friends, or "acquaintances," or "comrades" upon others, but he did not formulate and advocate a strategy based upon such data; it remained for Pickett and McGavran to achieve that. On the basis of his extensive observations and interview data, Wesley *does* counsel Methodists to share the gospel and not to wait until they are in the mood, or feel confident.

We have known many instances of this; Persons cold and dull, and scarce known how to believe their own words, have asserted, as they could, the truths of the gospel, and enforced them upon others, and at that very time God has caused light and love to spring up in their own hearts. Therefore, however you feel it in your own breast, speak as well as you can for God. Many times you will see some fruit upon others. (*Works*, Vol. 12, p. 359)

Mr. Wesley was acutely aware of the human relations sensitivities, skills, and approaches that are required for effective outreach. He gave to Methodist stewards the following instructions: "If you cannot relieve, do not grieve, the poor: Give them soft words, if nothing else: Abstain from either sour looks, or harsh words . . . . Put yourself in the place of every poor man; and deal with him as you would God should deal with you" (*Journal,* June 4, 1747).

Biographers tell how Wesley practiced his advice about compassionate listening, interesting conversation, being interested in people, and affirming human relations. Samuel Johnson complained, "I hate to meet John Wesley; the dog enchants you with his conversation, and then breaks away to go and visit some old woman!" One biographer recalls:

Once when Wesley and one of his itinerant preachers were taking lunch at a wealthy home, an incident occurred which showed the great man's tact. The daughter of the house, a beautiful girl, was much impressed with Mr. Wesley's preaching. While conversing with the young lady, Wesley's itinerant noticed that she was wearing a number of rings; holding her hand up for Mr. Wesley to see, he said, "What do you think of this, sir, for a Methodist's hand?" (Wesley's aversion for the wearing of jewelry was well known.) The girl blushed and no doubt felt ill at ease, but with characteristic poise Wesley only smiled and said, "The hand is very beautiful." The young lady appeared at the next service without her gems, and became a devoted Christian. (Parker, n.d., p. 26)

CHAPTER 5

Multiplying
Recruiting Units

In 1979, I visited the ruins of ancient Corinth. Our tour guide paused at the site of Corinth's first house church. She explained that it did not long remain the city's only house church; soon, there were perhaps a half dozen others. Someone voiced the inevitable question: "Why so many house churches? Wouldn't one have been enough?" Our guide replied, "No, one house church would not have been enough. Ancient Corinth in the New Testament period was new; many people of many tongues lived here, and their various religions and philosophies were competitive. Christianity might not have survived here if the Christian movement had confined its strength to the number of people who could gather in one house church. As they started more house churches, they were able to grow—and not without them. Besides," she said, "the second house church could reach some people the first could not, the third could reach still others, and so on."

Our group had been exposed to some excellent proven Church Growth theory, from a source who, presumably, had never read Wesley or McGavran. Only in recent years have we perceived what a large and multifaceted principle is involved here. Most earlier writers have addressed only part of the principle at a time. A more comprehensive thesis is now warranted: *There is a potent relationship between (a) the church's membership strength and growth and (b) the number, age, and*

mission of the church's "units"— at every level of the church's life.
This thesis includes four distinct principles.

First, and most obvious, there is a general correlation between a church's number of units (classes, choirs, groups, congregations, et al.) and its membership strength. This correlation is even observable in the life history of whole denominations. For example, the Reverend George Sails, former top executive of British Methodism's Department of Home Mission, was commenting on his church's consistent membership slide from 1923 through 1978. He also remarked that their number of congregations had declined in those years from about 15,000 to about 9,000, but he added that they had, in 1978, virtually the same number of members in each congregation (71, as I recall) as they had had in the denomination's strongest period! Thus, if the British Methodists had been starting churches at the same rate they were closing them, the denomination could still be experiencing an extended heyday.

Of course, the correlation between a denomination's membership strength and the number of its congregations is not always as precise as British Methodism's case, but the correlation is almost always strong. In one cluster of cases, *Asia Theological News* (July-September 1985, pp. 4 and 5) reported on the growth, in membership and number of congregations, of some Philippine denominations from 1971 through 1981:

Denomination	1971: Membership	Churches	1981: Membership	Churches
Christian and Missionary Alliance	22,527	368	70,000	1,037
Wesleyan Church	2,408	46	7,158	113
Nazarenes	937	24	6,009	109
Convention Baptist	34,429	302	56,000	541

Southern Baptist	15,048	161	61,040	722
Conservative Baptist	1,657	31	10,245	118
Lutheran Church	3,180	62	5,870	135

Clearly, all of the denominations experienced growth, and the increase in number of churches in each denomination was a significant factor in the denomination's growth. Yet, three of the denominations reported fewer members in each church in 1981 than in 1971: the Convention Baptists (114 to 103.5), the Southern Baptists (93.5 to 84.5), and the Lutheran Church (51.3 to 43.5). Two of the denominations reported more members in each church: the Christian and Missionary Alliance (61.2 to 67.5) and the Wesleyan Church (52.3 to 63.3). Two denominations reported significantly more members in each church: the Nazarenes (39 to 55) and the Conservative Baptists (53.5 to 86.8). So there are, understandably, variations within the general correlation between denominational membership strength and the number of churches in the denomination, but that this general correlation is one of the factors behind denominational growth or decline is beyond reasonable doubt.

There are many other principles involved in explaining (or planning) the trends of membership strength of churches, but this persistent correlation between denominational membership strength and number of churches (a principle that some folks regard as obvious) has a strategic importance too often ignored by denominational leaders. In the U. S. today, in most years, (1) the denominations that are growing are starting more churches than they are closing, (2) the denominations that are starting more churches than they are closing are growing, (3) the denominations that are declining in membership strength are closing more churches than they are starting, and (4) the denominations that are closing more churches than they are starting are declining. There ought to be a lesson in such a persistent correlation.

Sunday School Class Multiplication

I believe that Richard Myers, who taught Sociology of Religion at the Christian Theological Seminary in Indianapolis, was the first to demonstrate the validity of this principle in local churches, particularly regarding the number of classes in a Sunday school. In *Program Expansion: the Key to Church Growth,* privately published, Myers suggested three strong correlations from his research:

1. There is a correlation between the number of classes and the average attendance in a church school. In a church school, "The number of church school classes determined how many persons can participate in the church school. . . . More classes, larger attendance; fewer classes, smaller attendance. As the number of classes are increased or decreased, so does the attendance increase or decrease."

2. In churches, there is a correlation between program groups and church staff on the one hand and the church's overall membership strength on the other. Myers wrote that "congregations with the same number of program groups and church staff will have about the same church membership, worship attendance, and church school attendance, as well as women's society and youth fellowship groups."

3. There is a strong correlation between average Sunday school attendance and the number of people received into membership by profession of faith. Repeatedly, churches with about the same average Sunday school attendance report about the same number of professions of faith.

Myers believed that expansion of the Sunday school is a proven strategy for making new Christians, and he observed no ambiguous "hen and egg" relationship in all of this, for he knew which came first: *Because* you add classes and teachers and staff, the Sunday school attendance increases, and because attendance increases, the number received on profession of faith increases. Conversely, because you reduce the number of classes, attendance decreases, and, in time, professions of faith decline.

Two large Sunday schools can prove the principle for themselves. Suppose each Sunday school has an average adult division attendance of 100, distributed among 10 classes. Suppose Church A, campaigning for "efficiency" and "excellence," decides to merge its 10 classes into 5 larger classes so that all attenders will be led by one of the five best teachers. And suppose Church B mounts a campaign for outreach and growth and starts 10 new classes this season. A year from now, how will they compare in average attendance? Church A's approach will quietly have reduced the attendance from 100 to 70 or 80. In Church B's Sunday school, 4 of the 10 new classes will not have made it, but the other 6 will be thriving and prodding several of the older classes, resulting in an adult division average attendance of 130 to 140. Although those are my own estimates, not Myers', it was comparisons like these that convinced Myers that "the addition of classes is one of the keys to growth."

In comparing a strategy of merging classes with a strategy of adding classes, Myers discovered (as we all do) a world of trade-offs: It can be argued that the larger classes of Church A serve the present membership more effectively, but they are not as effective as the smaller classes of Church B "in bringing new people into its membership and then into the membership of the congregation." He saw the smaller classes and program groups, in which people can interact, and be missed, and form friendships, as much more prolific.

In the 1960s a number of churches took Myers' research and conclusions quite seriously. One, Myers reports, was First Methodist Church of Littleton, Colorado. In 1964 they had 12 classes (of all age groups), no more room, and, with their average Sunday school attendance of 400, they could not quite afford to build more space. They launched a second Sunday school session and started 12 new classes. They added a third session, and 12 more classes. They were now involving some 600 persons each Sunday, enough people to support a facilities expansion. They built 24 additional classrooms, and with 36 classrooms at their disposal they went to two sessions a Sunday and soon were averaging almost 1,000 in average Sunday school attendance.

Myers proclaimed growth possibilities through this principle in a period when such thinking was not fashionable, but that did not stop him from dreaming big. He speculated that if, in the Methodist Church, every congregation started just one new class in the next year, that would have an evangelical impact equivalent to starting 3,100 new congregations, and with no additional funding. Recently, Bishop Walter Underwood rediscovered this simple idea and challenged the United Methodist churches of Louisiana to start new classes. In 1984, the first year of this emphasis, they started more than 200 new Sunday school classes, and set bolder projections for the next year.

We have thus established two principles: (1) There is a correlation between the church's number of units and its membership strength, and (2) new units are, generally, more reproductive than old units. But how many units, or groups, should a church have? And how many should be new groups? This is best answered in terms of number of groups for every 100 members in the church, and my observations would suggest the following:

8 groups per 100 members—structured for significant growth.
7 groups per 100 members—structured for growth.
6 groups per 100 members—structured for maintenance to slight growth.
5 groups per 100 members—structured for maintenance or membership decline.
4 or fewer groups per 100 members—structured for decline.

Naturally, other principles affect the total results, such as: (a) whether a group's mission includes reaching new people, (b) whether many of the groups are relatively new, and (c) whether many groups relate to receptive target populations.

Win Arn's research conclusions are similar. He prescribes "at least seven groups in your church for every 100 members. The consequence of too few groups for members to build meaningful relationships is a high rate of inactives exiting through the back door." Arn also prescribes that one in five groups should be "new," that is, started within the past two years, since most groups have about an eighteen-month natural growth track, after which they lose some capacity to reach and assimilate new members. Arn agrees with Richard Myers that staffing for program growth and reaching people is crucial, prescribing that "your church should have one full-time staff member for every 150 persons in worship" (*The Win Arn Growth Report,* number 3). But other writers, such as Lyle Schaller in *The Multiple Staff and the Larger Church,* are discovering that many growing churches are dividing responsibilities of the staff two or three ways and hiring part-time staff who carry only one responsibility each, and that these part-time staff members are often more effective and economical.

In denominational growth, the ratio of new churches to the total number of churches is a proven factor. The natural growth track of new churches averages, say, fifteen years, during which they grow about 10 percent a year. Whether a denomination is growing or not is significantly influenced by the percentage of its congregations who are well planted and experiencing that first generation of growth. For instance, in the United States, the Southern Baptist Convention (with about 35,000 churches) and the United Methodist Church (with about 38,000) both have, at this writing, a similar number of congregations. But the United Methodists (because church extension was not fashionable for much of the 1960s and 1970s) have only about 600 churches in that first generation growth track. The Southern Baptists have about 9,000! The effectiveness of the Southern Baptists in (1) new church planting and (2) Sunday school growth (and United Methodism's lower effectiveness in these two areas) are the two most important explanations for the growth of the Southern Baptist Convention in a generation of United Methodism's net membership decline of almost two million members.

A third principle may now be suggested: Sometimes, old units flanked by a new growing unit will again experience growth. In a church where I consulted, the one Sunday school class for couples with young children was closed to outsiders. They had met for three years, had shared some struggles, and had become good friends and a cohesive group—but were experienced by most visiting couples as a clique. Some forty couples had visited over the past couple of years, and most had not returned. There were three exceptions: A very attractive couple had been spontaneously included by the group, a socially aggressive couple had broken in to the fellowship, and a couple already known well by several member couples had been effectively included. All others felt ignored, frozen out, or not really wanted. I recommended that the church start a new, second class for couples with young children—to meet in the available space right across the hall from the first group. Several couples who had visited the first class became the nucleus of the new class. This new class experienced significant growth, and the first class observed all this apostolic activity right across the hall. The first class did a self-study and determined that their closeness *did* have unintended effects on visitors. They devised several ways to be more open to visitors and once more began growing.

Fourth, old units that help new units get started sometimes experience new growth. In one city, Eastside Church felt they had grown to about the "right size." They chose to grow no more, and for more than a year they didn't. But they recognized their apostolic obligation, and they helped a new congregation get started. The new congregation thrived, but Eastside Church caught "apostolic fever" in this involvement with the new church, and Eastside started growing again, despite their earlier resolve.

The Southern Baptists of the U. S. have long been familiar with such strategic knowledge, and thus have built the largest Sunday school system in the history of Protestant Christianity, with more than 3.5 million persons meeting in some class each Sunday morning. In the 1960s, they experienced a period of decline like other mainline denominations were experiencing, but they did the research and strategic planning necessary to become a growing Sunday school movement once again. In the research, they studied the earlier strategies within their own history and rediscovered the 1920s emphases of a Reverend Arthur Flake and his "Flake Formula" for Sunday school growth. Some churches had not forgotten it, and the research of Andrew Anderson (1976) showed that "perhaps with no exception, churches that use it consciously and persistently experience growth." The Flake Formula for Sunday school growth was cogently stated:

1. Locate the prospects.
2. Enlarge the organization.
3. Enlist and train the workers.
4. Provide the space.
5. Go after the people.

There is, of course, nothing peculiarly Baptist (or even Christian) about the formula. Flake simply delineated the generic steps that any organization might take in managing its expansion. For instance, in this time of a declining post–high school population in the United States, a liberal arts college could follow that formula to ensure its own survival, growth, and continued contribution.

In recent years the Baptists have added to this inherited formula, making it even more effective: (1) They now execute the strategy each quarter (whereas Flake had called for an annual execution). Each fall, winter, spring, and summer, participating Southern Baptist churches are intentionally locating prospects, enlarging the organization, enlisting and training new teachers, locating or providing space for new classes, and inviting people. (2) The Baptists now emphasize Sunday school expansion through multiplying many new small Sunday school classes, small enough for people to minister to one another as well as study the Scriptures. Their experience shows that, of the people enrolled in a Sunday school class, average Sunday attendance will be about half that number. So, (3) part of their thrust is to enroll as many people as possible. They have found that many unchurched people are "inoculated," at least for the moment, against joining someone's church; but these people do not, generally, have comparable hang-ups about joining a group or a class. And (4) in each church, one person is responsible for recruiting and training new teachers for the new classes that will be created. For the first five weeks of each quarter, this person observes maturing Christians in the Sunday school and invites teachers and other leaders to point to likely candidates. For the next eight weeks of that quarter, this officer teaches a class for the new prospective teachers.

The Baptists have discovered that these proliferating new classes serve as effective recruiting groups and ports of entry into faith and into the church itself. They have discovered that those who join a church by this route are already assimilated, and therefore much less likely to drop out. They have also discovered that as Sunday school attendance increases, so does worship attendance.

The principle of multiplying units to reach people is more easily available to churches than even most growing churches have perceived. Most growing churches are growing through multiplying Sunday school classes, and frequently through multiplying women's circles, but (1) most growing churches do not think to multiply redemptive cells for men. They limit their outreach potential to what one organized men's fellowship can achieve. (2) Most churches provide only one organized fellowship for senior high youth, and most teenage visitors to a single option youth fellowship do not "stick," reporting in interviews that "I didn't fit in" or "they weren't my type." But the churches that multiply options for teenagers, and invite teenagers to participate in developing a new youth group, are experiencing powerful growth in their youth ministries. (3) I am amazed at how many churches provide only one worship service. This is usually rationalized by the expression, "The worship service we have now isn't usually full." That may be true, but not really significant. For instance, if it is 80 percent full it looks full to first-time visitors. It looks full on the Sundays (like Easter) when the church is most likely to have visitors. Besides, there are no compelling reasons why the committee that once designed a church's present sanctuary should, *de facto,* be controlling the number of worship services a church now offers. Most churches who start a second (or third, or fourth) worship service experience at least a 10 percent net increase in their total weekly worship attendance (and 10 percent more with each additional option). So, in many ways, as we multiply options for people we are able to include and involve more people.

Wesley's Multiplying "Classes"

As mentioned earlier, John Wesley promoted the multiplication of the redemptive cells he called "classes," and this strategy was crucial to the expansion of the eighteenth-century Methodist movement. "Preach in as many places as you can. Start as many classes as you can. Do not preach without starting new classes." This strategy has slipped into neglect over two centuries, and today's church needs to rediscover Wesley's wisdom.

Wesley taught, for instance, that new classes and societies need shepherding, and that it is *not* faithful or productive to start more units than the movement can manage. He did not advocate rash and frenetic starting of cells and societies. He saw no virtue in starting new ministry or group life that dies soon after birth, or is stunted in growth.

Whenever any are awakened, you will do well to join them together immediately. But I *do not* advise you to *go* on *too fast. It is not expedient to break up more ground than you can keep;* to preach at any more places than you or your brethren can constantly attend. To preach once in a place, and no more, very seldom does any good; it only alarms the devil and his children, and makes them more upon their guard against a first assault. (*Works,* Vol. 13, p. 71, emphasis added)

Will [the societies] prosper as well when they are left as sheep without a shepherd? The experiment has been tried again and again; and always with the same event: Even the strong in faith grow weak and faint; many of the weak made shipwreck of the faith; the awakened fell asleep; sinners, changed for a while, returned as a dog to the vomit. (*Works,* Vol. 13, p. 200)

All worthwhile ministry must be effectively managed. Indeed, the rich and growing writing on management should be seen as a cousin of Church Growth writing and necessary reading for the Church Growth leader. The growth of Methodism in eighteenth-century Britain was impressive, but not uncontrolled, stampeding growth. Howard Snyder reports that, "After thirty years, in 1768, Methodism had 40 circuits and 27,341 members. Ten years later the numbers had grown to 60 circuits and 40,089 members; in another decade, 99 circuits and 66,375 members. By 1798, seven years after Wesley's death, the totals had jumped to 149 circuits with 101,712 members" (Snyder, 1980, p. 54).

Wesley's deeper contribution comes from his agenda for

the class meetings. Indeed, the class meeting agenda was the means to "spread the power of Jesus' name." This is an imperative place to focus, because this generation's church naively assumes that "a small group is a small group is a small group." Like waves in the Atlantic, "If you have seen one, you have seen them all." Church leaders are apt to respond to *any* proposal for ministry through small groups with "We have already done that," or "We already have those"—assuming, again, that any two groups are the same, so if you have seen one you have seen (and understand) the other.

But the assumption does not bear examination. Football, baseball, and soccer are each played in stadiums, in front of fans, between two teams wearing uniforms and contesting over a ball, but no one believes the three sports are identical. A Communist cell meeting and a group therapy session both take place in a group and it may appear, at a glance, that "the same thing" is going on both places, but perhaps the only thing they have in common is that they interact and pursue their respective agendas in a small group. Wesley's classes (and their message for Church Growth in our time) should be understood by looking at their agenda, and should not be casually confused with any other small group we may be familiar with. To be specific, the class meetings were *not* "Bible study groups," or "prayer groups," or "sharing groups," or "sensitivity groups," or "therapy groups," or "rap sessions," or anything else that most churches have. Then what were the classes, and what was allegedly special about them?

In some ways, Wesley's multiplying class meetings were remarkably simple. They were specific groups within a Methodist "society," and several societies were arranged, for the sake of effective management, into a "circuit." About twelve persons met in a class, led by a layperson, either male or (more often) female. There was only one requirement for joining: One had to be "awakened," expressing now the desire "to flee the wrath to come," to experience God's forgiveness and his power for a new life. Wesley devised some remarkably lucid standards for his new life, which were not the heart of that life, but served as its backbone, and as the foundation of the group's ministry. People who joined promised (with the group's help) to (1) "do good," (2) "avoid all known sin," and (3) pursue regularly "the means of grace" (Scripture reading, daily prayer, the Lord's supper, fasting, and regular worship at the parish church). They came, weekly, to the class meeting and reported, in turn, their activities and behaviors of the past week in regard to those three vows. Their peers responded to these reports, with "encouragement or rebuke or advice" (Luccock, 1964, p. 25) as appropriate. Members were taught to expect, in God's good time, to experience their justification. One first joined a class and then, in three months, the Methodist society. One could remain a member for as long as there was continued evidence of the desire for justification and new life. In time, two years on the average, most members experienced justification and new birth; and from that point on they "expected" to experience "sanctification," that is, "being made perfect in love" in this life.

But, because eighteenth-century Methodism's experience took place in a different time and culture from our own, the deeper meaning or mission of the class meetings is not so obvious today, and at least several scholars have tried to pinpoint it. Gloster Udy's pioneering scholarship (1962) concluded, most of all, that the mission of the class meetings was to provide people with the kind of family experience that the upheaval and fragmenting of the industrial revolution had robbed from them. The class experiences inculcated interpersonal values and facilitated people's growth and development. Udy features quotations from Wesley, such as the following, which emphasize

that Christian fellowship of which they had not so much an idea before. They began to "bear one another's burdens" and naturally to "care for each other." As they had daily a more intimate acquaintance with, so they had a more endeared affection for, each other. And, "speaking the truth in love, they grew up into Him all things." (Quoted in Udy, 1962, p. 28)

Udy found great significance in the powerful verbs that Wesley employed in one version of his directions to the classes: "You are 'taught of God not to forsake the assembly of yourselves together, as the manner of some is, but to instruct, admonish, exhort, reprove, comfort, confirm, and in every way build up one another' " (see Udy, 1962, pp. 40-46).

Udy believes that the class meeting was Wesley's practical expression of his conviction that Christianity is "not a solitary religion" but a social faith. Udy believes that some appropriate form of the class meeting is the means of change in our own generation and culture.

David Lowes Watson (1984) finds great significance in the fact that class meeting participants held one another *accountable* for living by the three vows. The very fact that I voluntarily report weekly to my peers "breaks the tyranny of moods." Every person does good and avoids evil when he or she is in the mood, and does not when in a contrary mood! Most people are driven by their "moods." But when, in a life situation, a Methodist's mood is not conducive to doing good, and he or she can recall the promise to report shortcomings, that energizes the person to do the deed anyway. Often the mood accompanies (rather than precedes) the deed, and the member reports to the class a moral victory. Watson suggests that humans are most successful in important pursuits when they use an accountable team approach, and recalls an analogy from his own college days:

It came home to me many years ago when I was a student at Oxford University. Like most new students, I arrived with all sorts of good resolutions, . . . [and] . . . one . . . was that I was going to keep physically fit, and I decided that a good way to do this would be to go for a run each morning before breakfast. The first week, I ran every morning. Breakfast took on new meaning, and I felt invigorated and refreshed for the day's work. The second week, I missed a couple of mornings. The third week, I missed all but one morning. The fourth week I missed altogether, and the fifth week I made an amended resolution—that *next* year I would go running each morning.

The following year, however, I took a precautionary measure. I asked the person next door if he would like to go running with me. "Good idea," he said. And with somewhat mixed feelings, I knew I was committed. On the days I was late, he would bang on my door with a cheery word: "Time to be going!" There were several mornings, by no means as many, when I would return him the favor. Occasionally, we would both be late, and would spring out of our rooms simultaneously, insisting that we were just about to come and get the other! We made it through the year, every morning. (Watson, 1984, pp. 11-12)

My own conclusions differ from Watson's only in connotation and emphasis. What is involved in Wesley's redemptive cells is not as legalistic as the word *accountability* connotes and is not the stoic British slug-it-out kind of discipline that Watson's analogy might suggest. Rather, the interaction within such cells, based on common clear objectives for member's lives and group support in pursuit of them, is energizing and is not so much a discipline as a liberation.

Perhaps an incident out of my own exercise regimen will clarify my point. I "pump iron" for fitness, and when I am at home I work out in late afternoon in my home gym while listening to "All Things Considered" or "Prairie Home Companion" on National Public Radio. Some afternoon workouts are, indeed, a joyless tough-it-out-hour. But when I travel, I work out in gyms and health clubs. One afternoon while doing a consulting project for Fuller Theological Seminary, I felt in need of a workout. I remembered that a health club owned and managed by a Mr. Universe was not too far away. Upon walking out of the locker room, appropriately attired, I was greeted by a half dozen perspiring workout enthusiasts. We exchanged names, and one of them commented, "We pull together here." I decided to begin with "bench presses" and loaded enough weight onto a racked barbell to permit me to lift it eight times, nine on a "good day." As I reclined on the bench, one fellow spontaneously stopped by to "spot" me. I squeezed out ten rounds. He said, "more." I responded with number eleven, and with his hands under the bar, managed a twelfth. The gym is coed. A very healthy younger woman breezed by en route to an exercise station. I did two more! I spent the whole hour and a half "overachieving." On reflection, I was not overachieving. Rather, the experience of that serious intentional fellowship, pulling together to achieve common objectives, had pulled out of me more than I knew was there, and helped me to identify and achieve more of my potential. I was stronger in, and because of, that fellowship than I could have been alone.

As Watson suggests, there are many secular analogies today of the Wesleyan class meeting's dynamic. For instance, the wide experience of Alcoholics Anonymous tells us that when alcoholics pull together, hold one another to the sobriety standard, and encourage one another, they attain objectives they lack the power to achieve alone. In Weight Watchers, thousands of people who could not trim their weight alone have been able to do so when fortified by the challenges and cheering of their peers. And leaders of Group Dynamics will recognize, in the Wesleyan class meetings, a proven mechanism for achieving change in people. Hal Luccock was right: "The class meeting represented a disciplined fellowship for mutual help" (Luccock, 1964, p. 25). More specifically I suggest that members helped each other to achieve a shared objective: *to live as Christians.*

This clear objective raises one annoying question: Most of the people who joined a Methodist class were not yet Christians who had experienced God's grace. They were "awakened" seekers. How could people who were not yet Christians *live* as Christians? They couldn't! True, the accountability system enabled people to "do good" on hundreds of occasions when, without peer support, they would not have. Indeed, compared to their secular counterparts, some of them lived extraordinary lives and became extraordinary people.

But they also blew it time and again. Despite their resolve, the support of their peers, and the weekly reporting, they still failed countless times to attain their clear standards and objectives. Mr. Wesley knew this, and I believe that Wesley knew that their repeated experience of falling short of the clear (and seemingly attainable) goals would, in measurable time, help them realize their need for God's grace in order to live like that, and would open them to his seeking, accepting, empowering grace. Wesley, I'm guessing, had developed the class experience to replicate in other people his own pilgrimage of trying his best to live as a Christian, and often failing, which had opened him to the grace of God.

Howard Snyder's *The Radical Wesley* suggests an even more revolutionary agenda for Wesley's class meetings, a point worth amplifying here. Wesley was an astute student of "the primitive church" as reflected in the New Testament, particularly the pastoral epistles. He was also an astute observer of the eighteenth-century Church of England. He saw the primitive church's contagious compassion, powerful faith, unswerving hope, daring apostolic courage, and vision for humanity. He did not see that kind of love, faith, hope, courage, and vision in his generation's established church. Indeed, Wesley came to see the Church of England as a "fallen church," because for him "true apostolic succession came to mean . . . the continuity of apostolic spirit and witness in the Christian community" (Snyder, 1980, p. 82).

Wesley also observed that certain normative behaviors were characteristic of life in the primitive church. They met together "to stir up one another to love and good works . . . encouraging one another" (Heb. 10:24-25). They seemed to have taught, admonished, exhorted, and prayed for one another. They rejoiced with those who rejoiced, and wept with those who wept (Rom. 12:15). Their behaviors toward one another ranged from telling one's sins to another (Matt. 18:15-18) to building one another up (I Thess. 5:11). And Wesley believed the earliest churches followed the script of James (5:16): "Confess your sins to one another, and pray for one another, that you may be healed." With regret, Wesley did not see such behavior in his Anglican Church. One of the causes of this, he believed, was the lack of small groups, a deficiency not present in the early church's house churches.

Wesley ventured a revolutionary hypothesis: that the occurrence of the first phenomenon (faith, hope, power, etc.) depends on the second. That is, as you gather Christians and seekers together to confess their sins, encourage one another, rejoice together, and so forth, the life, love, faith, hope, and power of the Apostolic church emerges. He sensed that if he drew people together in cells to challenge and encourage each other to live daily as Christians, that, through their protracted experiences, the contagion and power of the Apostolic church would move in human history once again. And it happened! Wesley offers today's churches and Church Growth writings something far more powerful than merely another crack at "small groups" in the way these are usually (mis)understood. Churches that multiply Wesley's kind of groups will grow with power.

It should be noted that some of Wesley's own contemporaries, including George Whitefield, did not understand Wesley's agenda in the class meetings. This makes Whitefield's confession, near the end of his career and life, doubly tragic and explains why his preaching facilitated many decisions but no enduring movement: "My brother Wesley acted wisely. The souls that were awakened under his ministry he joined in class, and thus preserved the fruit of his labours. This I neglected, and my people are a rope of sand" (quoted in Ayling, 1979, p. 201). The statement reveals that Whitefield regarded Wesley's classes and his other structures for redemptive fellowship as merely a means of preserving the victories of preaching. But for Wesley, preaching and public witness were mere preamble. The redemptive action took place in the lay led class meetings, and in people's hearts. The class meetings were Wesley's strategy for helping people to become the people they were born to be and deeply within themselves had always wanted to be. The achievements of this strategy reveal Wesley as a spiritual brother of the man of La Mancha (Don Quixote), who saw that "too much sanity may be madness, and the maddest of all [is] to see life as it is and not as it should be."

Wesley understood Christianity as "no solitary religion," but as "a social religion" in which the reality and "power of Jesus' name" were especially present within the fellowship of people pulling together to live as Christians. Four principles are involved in this affirmation:

1. The power is available to awaken people in any setting; to awaken people and enroll them in classes were the two objectives in field preaching and the witness of laity.

2. Awakened people experience grace and faith from the ministry of the cells—sometimes in a class meeting or society worship, but more often in their solitude in the hours following a meeting.

3. Once gained, faith is maintained within the fellowship of class and society. Wesley observed that people

who, for whatever reasons, dropped out of the fellowship, typically experienced the erosion of faith.

4. People also grow toward completeness in Christian love within the fellowships, especially a second type of cell called the "bands," which Wesley created for people serious about "moving on toward perfection."

Multiplying Units Today

Remarkable and strong church growth is possible using the many avenues of the "multiplication of units" strategy. It is not an easy Church Growth strategy to master compared, say, to the social bridges strategy, because a number of management competencies are required to execute it. And it is not an easy strategy to learn to execute, although people and churches who already know how find it increasingly prolific. For instance, while leading some Church Growth training several years ago in Charlotte, North Carolina, I was apprised of the contrasting experiences of two prominent denominations. The first had not started a new congregation in that judicatory for twenty years. Now they wanted to start one, but they were asking, How do you go about it? Where do you start? How do you decide where to locate one? What kinds of skills does the founding pastor need? Where do you find a pastor like that? Where can we find the money for a new church? No one has any experience! Several judicatory meetings had dragged on for many frustrating hours. On the other hand, the other denomination had started one to three congregations a year for twenty years in that section of North Carolina. They had a reservoir of models and experienced people. They were not awed or intimidated by new church planting. Informed answers to "how you go about it" and "where you go for help" and "how to raise up and train new leadership" were part of their common folklore. Their judicatory meetings involved projections and goals, reports of plans and achievements, brief discussions and stories of what God was doing, and their meetings finished on time.

This entrepreneurial task is eminently worth learning, and Win and Charles Arn have prescribed "nine simple steps to starting new groups in your church" (1982, p. 167) for church planners and leaders who do have to begin at the beginning:

1. Define the target group of people to minister to.

2. Research the target audience and the kind of ministry that would possibly respond to their particular needs.

3. Find a committed lay person/s willing to be involved in starting such a new group. The person should be similar to the target group.

4. Train this person in the logistics of starting a new group.

5. Begin the recruiting process prior to the first group session.

6. Find an appropriate meeting place.

7. Stress the importance of the first several months. They are critical to the success of the group.

8. Keep accurate records of the experience for reference in starting later groups.

9. Build in monitoring and evaluation procedures for the first nine months.

The world's most exceptional case study of church growth through the multiplication of units is Yoido Central Full Gospel Church of Seoul, Korea. Back in 1974 they had "only" 20,000 members. But by April 1986, the church had 510,000 members and was filling the sanctuary (with a capacity of 20,000) seven times each Sunday, and overflow crowds in up to a dozen satellite sanctuaries were participating by closed circuit television! How have they grown? Through the deliberate spawning of more than 50,000 "home cell groups" in Metropolitan Seoul. This cell life is managed through nineteen "divisions." Each cell is lay led, the leaders receive continual training at the central church, and each thirty cells receive supervision from a pastor on Yoido Church's (extensive) pastoral staff.

Not many of us identify with such an awesome achievement; it staggers the imagination. But, because of this case, there is no known limit to the membership strength a church can attain using the multiplication of units strategy—providing the leaders have the vision, competency, and energy to manage an expanding enterprise.

Ministering to People's Needs

The secular world knows, or expects, that whatever else churches do, they minister, especially to people with needs. If no other part of Christianity's image is clear, that part is clear, and valid. Our Lord reported that he came "not to be served, but to serve," and he calls his church to this ministry. He dramatized this life-style by washing his disciples' feet, and together they healed the deaf and blind, liberated the oppressed and possessed, empowered lame persons to "rise up and walk," cared for the poor, and cleansed lepers. The world's only worldwide network of programmatic compassion began quite early in the history of the Christian movement.

Compassionate ministry to people's needs was at the heart of eighteenth-century Methodism. Mr. Wesley informed ministries to human needs using essentially the same data-based approach that informed Methodist evangelization. He made "a study of souls," and of the ministries that help souls and set them free from sin and free them in the midst of suffering. Martin Schmidt tells us of Wesley's "confidence in the potency of fact," (1973, p. 124) and emphasizes "Wesley's respect for the facts as the first principle behind his pastoral care" (p. 128). To obtain the facts, Wesley visited, observed, interviewed, and corresponded with people in sundry conditions. He visited persons who were possessed, obsessed, and oppressed. He visited persons in prison, persons who had seizures, prisoners on death row, sick persons, anxious persons, guilt-stricken persons, grieving persons, persons on their death beds. In each situation, he was there to minister, but also to gather data. He studied souls through lengthy correspondences with a number of people, especially women who were local leaders across the movement. He corresponded with a Sarah Crosby for thirty-two years. As he had done with his evangelism data, he collected his recorded observations, important letters, cases, and so forth in his journal, which he reviewed. He gradually systematized his insights into a pastoral theology, which in turn informed his pastoral practice, advice, and training.

He "programmed" these insights into the structure of Methodism and the training of leaders, and produced a movement distinctive for its preaching and its pastoral care. The class meeting, of course, was established to help awakened struggling people find their way. The society, too, "was erected for purposes of pastoral care and secured its permanence" (Schmidt, 1973, p. 118). Pastoral care was the responsibility of the whole fellowship. As Wesley had great confidence in laypersons to do the work of evangelists, so he confidently vested laypeople with many ministries to persons with needs. He charged a society member

frequently, nay constantly, to visit the poor, the widow, the sick, the fatherless, in their affliction. . . . It is true, this is not pleasing to flesh and blood. There are a thousand circumstances usually attending it which shock the delicacy of our nature, or rather our education. But yet, the blessing which follows this labour of love will more than balance the cross. (*Works*, Vol. 12, p. 302)

Wesley also devised some institutionalized approaches to assist poor people. He established a fund for poor people to obtain small interest-free loans to survive emergencies. He opened a dispensary for the poor and established a home for aged persons and infirm widows. He established a school for poor children at Kingswood, near Bristol, and another at Moorsfield, in London. Stanley Ayling (1979, p. 167) reports that Wesley knew he was only helping a minute fraction of the people who needed help, and quotes him acknowledging that "it is certain we have barely the first outlines of a plan with regard to temporals," but Wesley knew he dare not become absorbed in institutional work for the poor, lest the even greater apostolic priority be neglected.

Wesley espoused special convictions about Methodism's ministry to persons experiencing sickness. Schmidt explains that "during hospital visits [Wesley] was occasionally asked by patients in adjacent beds to pray with them or to conduct a service of worship. During these visits he came to realize the general importance and the spiritual nature of ministering to people in the hospital" (1973, pp. 127-28).

Wesley installed the office of "sick visitor" in each society, and emphasized its importance. He saw that sick people were frequently receptive to spiritual conversation; indeed, he saw hospitals as fields ready for harvesting by Methodist lay ministry. Many sick people got well, and found their way into faith and Methodism.

In much of Christian history, however, the relationship between the church's caring ministries and her evangelistic ministry has not been adequately explored or understood. Most Christians have (mis)perceived these ministries as two disparate expressions of the church's mission, and some have taken sides on which one they think is really important. In most mainline Protestant churches today, much more ministry takes place than evangelism; evangelism is reserved for Christians who are "that type." Most mainline Protestant leaders have never discovered that "they also serve who evangelize"; in other words, they do not realize that to introduce people to Christ and invite them to respond and become disciples *is* a serving ministry. In fact, the reasons supporting a closer relationship between ministry and evangelism (and social reform and evangelism) are rather obvious and compelling, but I am astonished at how few Christians have ever considered the following points:

1. In most societies, the church's service and compassionate ministries provide the credibility for its message. Most people do not find believable, or worth considering, the message of a church that, as far as they know, "just preaches."

2. As we shall see, some facets of the church's gospel are better communicated through the church's service *(diakonia)* or fellowship *(koinonia)* than merely through proclamation *(kerygma)*.

3. Involving new disciples in caring ministries is a necessary phase of their conversion, enabling the gospel to be incarnated in their personalities and life-styles, and not confined to the cognitive and affective parts of their personalities. True discipleship is, finally, behavioral.

4. In regard to cross-cultural service, the church really has just two options: (a) Raise up enough indigenous converts for them to (more effectively) minister to their people, or (b) keep sending (less effective) cross-cultural servants and thereby keep the recipient population dependent on the sending population. (The critics of mission, incidentally, complain in either case: If missionaries convert some of the people, it is labeled "imperialism"; if they do not raise up a strong indigenous church but continue serving, it is labeled "paternalism.")

5. The legitimate social reform objectives of the church in any society are only achieved when the movement recruits and develops a sufficiently large number of disciples to pursue social objectives effectively. Evangelism provides the personnel for Christ's whole mission in the world. People only become involved in ministry, social reform, and witness as they experience grace, join the messianic community, and come to share God's own dream of the Kingdom that is to be.

6. By means of "redemption and lift," that is, the rise in dignity, self-esteem, education, and hope that accompanies most any people's experience of being evangelized and discipled, faithful evangelism may be the most effective single proven method of liberating people from disadvantage and oppression and for reforming a society.

7. There is an inevitable relationship between attaining a just society and fashioning some just people within that society. Without doubt the relationship is reciprocal: A just society provides a climate that makes Christianity's message believable, that is, congruent with some of the people's experiences in that just society; and a society is more likely to approximate justice when some community is modeling justice and producing altruistic people who work for justice. Logically, an effective movement for justice in any society has to begin with enough justice-seeking persons.

Theological Rationale

A passage in Luke 5:12-14 dramatizes these connections and suggests the theological rationale behind ministries to people with needs. A man "full of leprosy" approached Jesus, fell on his knees, and implored, "Lord, if you will, you can make me clean." Jesus responded with a touch, saying "I will; be clean." The man was thus cleansed, and Jesus directed him to go to the temple (as prescribed in Leviticus 14) and have the authorized priest formally declare him a leper no longer.

Leprosy was the most dreaded disease in ancient societies. The physical symptoms were bad enough. In one form, sores festered and spread, and eventually one lost some fingers or toes. A second form attacked the central nervous system, and eventually the afflicted person would lose all feeling in an arm or leg. Yet the worst effects of each form were deferred for ten or twenty years. We know, from the cases of millions of people who continue smoking though aware of its later consequences, that people do not fear afflictions whose worst effects are for years deferred. Yet, when a person contracted leprosy, it was an immediate and enormous crisis. Why?

Leprosy was dreaded because of the mountain of problems that went with it. Imagine a scene in the earlier life of the man in Luke 5. He noticed a white spot on his upper arm one day. His wife found another on his back. He knew what it might be and walked to the temple to present himself for inspection to the priest who checked people for diseases like leprosy. The priest nodded. He had seen these symptoms too many times to be mistaken and said, "I now declare you to be a leper." At that moment, the man's whole life changed. As prescribed in Leviticus 13, he tore his clothes and mussed his hair. With hand over lips, he exited into the courtyard, calling out "Unclean! Unclean!" and saw the people scatter in horror or disgust. Never again would he return to his home, or kiss his wife, or hug his children, or shake the hands of his old friends, or work at his trade, or worship in the synagogue. He would now live alone or in a small colony with other lepers, outside the city walls, perhaps in a cave.

In modern terms, he was now a "loser" with no future. He would be ignored, or feared, or loathed, and "kept in his place," a second-class citizen. In time his self-esteem would sink, for we all reflect the appraisal of others; he would feel unwanted and would loathe himself.

We are told that, in another miracle of modern medicine, leprosy, or Hansen's disease, has been all but wiped out across the earth, and that lepers are a vanishing people. Maybe, but in terms of its social harm—the most dreaded part of the condition—our age is afflicting more people with "leprosy" than ever before. I doubt that there have ever been more second-class citizens, who see no doors of opportunity and feel they have no future. Robert Schuller has reminded us that low self-esteem is epidemic in Western society.

What are the causes of today's widespread "social leprosy"? Some of it, undoubtably, is a self-inflicted wound arising from sloth, or drinking, or drug abuse, or overeating, or missed opportunities, or a hundred other mentionables. But it is also inflicted by others, as ethnic minorities, women, Vietnam war veterans, aging people, people with handicapping conditions, and others have rightly protested. I am embarrassed to report that the church does not yet transcend its surrounding cultures. The church is as likely as any other institution to inflict social leprosy—usually disenfranchising and excluding people by stereotyping them and affixing theological labels.

Regardless of the causes, the church today is called to reaffirm the mission of Jesus and the earliest apostolic church in a mission to lepers, and it needs a strategy for identifying the lepers' colonies in a mass society and for ministering to marginal and low-self-esteem people. In other words, the church is called to be an extension of its Lord's incarnation, compassionately responsive to the needs of hurting people. I will be suggesting that the church can effectively pursue such an agenda today through, of all things, an informed *marketing strategy!*

But first, one more theological criterion needs unpacking: Effective evangelism takes place through *kerygma, koinonia,* and *diakonia,* three terms from the Greek New Testament translated as message, fellowship, and service. (*See* Hunter, 1979, pp. 29ff.)

Most Christians know that evangelism involves *kerygma,* communicating the message. Jesus and the apostles were all oral communicators of the glad tidings of God's promised Kingdom. Paul declared that "it pleased God through the folly of what we preach to save those who believe" (I Cor. 1:21). In this secular age, in which many people have no understanding of Christianity, the gospel must be taught. Yet, people are more than "souls with ears."

Koinonia, the redemptive power of contagious Christian fellowship, is also indispensable to effective evangelism. Donald McGavran has observed that "we do not live in a world in which even-handed exploration of the truth goes on in a climate cooly impartial to all beliefs" (Montgomery and McGavran, 1980, p. 31). Rather, as Donald Soper has often observed, "By *kerygma,* the Christian faith is taught; by *koinonia,* the Christian faith is caught." Kenneth Scott Latourette, in the first volume of his *History of the Expansion of Christianity,* contends that the early church probably attracted as many people through the power of its fellowship, a fellowship open to anyone, as it did through its oral proclamation. John Wesley's class meetings and societies recaptured this dynamic in eighteenth-century England.

Diakonia, as suggested above, is intrinsic to evangelism's effectiveness for at least two reasons. First, people decide that the message of a serving and justice-seeking church is credible. Second, new believers become actual disciples as they follow Christ in caring service.

To summarize: By *kerygma* the Christian faith is taught, by *koinonia* the Christian faith is caught, by *diakonia* the Christian faith is bought. Jesus' word and life is mediated through the church's message, fellowship, and service. People are not living as Christians unless they are involved in loving relations, service, and ministry. To make this possible, the authentic evangelical church offers varied ministry opportunities for all of its people.

These three resources of the gospel correspond, naturally, to how people respond in order to accept God's invitation appropriately. They engage in four turnings that are part of becoming a Christian (*see* Hunter, 1979, pp. 31-32). From missionary leaders like D. T. Niles and Stephen Neill, we have learned that people become Christians when they turn toward, and become faithfully involved with: (1) Christ, (2) the gospel, (3) the church, and (4) the world. From lengthy observations of new Christians and those becoming Christians, it is important to know that the four turnings generally take place one at a time in a person's life, but in any conceivable order.

The Marketing Approach

The marketing approach, as presented in Philip Kotler's splendid text *Marketing for Nonprofit Organizations* (1982), delineates ways that any organization, including a church, can identify "markets" or subcultures of humanity, discover their unmet felt needs, and develop services or products that meet those needs in exchange for their payment, support, or membership. The church can strengthen its effectiveness in ministry by the methods of marketing, and even more by facing the kinds of questions that marketing people ask.

Question One: Is a congregation going to be responsive or unresponsive to the needs of unchurched people in its area of ministry? To be sure, most any church started out responsive to the people in its environment. It attracted some of these people, met their needs, they joined the church, and the church grew. As the church grew, the pastor and other leaders necessarily focused inward more and more on nurturing and activating its growing membership. Roman Catholic missiologists refer to this phenomenon as the "choke law" of missionary work, that is, the priority of the pastoral work needed for growing numbers of Christians chokes out the possibility of further evangelization (Donovan, 1978, p. 99). Meanwhile, the community around the church was changing. Some people moved out and other types of people moved in, and the folks that stayed experienced life's natural stages and their needs changed. The result is an increasingly irrelevant church, no longer scratching where most of the unchurched people itch, and increasingly perceived as unresponsive to their needs and life situations.

Question Two: Does a congregation intend to be a selling church or a marketing church? A classic example of this involves two companies in Detroit, in the 1920s, the Ace Buggy Whip Company and the Ford Transportation Company. Each company, at the time, manufactured buggy whips, but the two companies saw their main business differently. Ace saw their business as selling buggy whips; Ford saw their business as providing personal transportation for people. The way they defined their business determined whether they discerned the signs of the times. Ace tried harder and harder, in vain, to sell buggy whips to people, who now wanted cars, while Ford was leading the automobile revolution in the middle-class market.

In one community, St. John's Church is still pushing "buggy whips"—the Bible in Elizabethan English, eighteenth-century German pipe organ music, and potluck suppers for traditional nuclear families. Unchurched people are not responding; the church has decided there is something "wrong" with these people. Trinity Church, in the same community, is growing. They surveyed their community and interviewed a lot of people. Then they started using the Good News Bible, "even in church." They launched a ministry to single parents, began an after-school ministry for children of working parents, and recently a guitar appeared at the 11:00 A.M. worship service! "Market-oriented" churches discover people's actual needs, relate the resources of the gospel to their needs, and adapt their ministries to fit the people they are called to reach.

A word of caution is appropriate: the marketing model is *not* a perfect model for the church, for at least four reasons: (1) A church can become excessively responsive, to the point of "letting the world write its agenda." When that happens, the church has forgotten to be steward of God's revealed agenda, and becomes a hijacked front organization for some other cause. (2) The church's relationship with undiscipled people cannot duplicate the "exchange" part of the marketing model. We are called to follow our Lord in compassionate goodwill for people even if they never respond to grace and become disciples. But we are closer to "exchange" than we assume, since we can only help people who avail themselves of the help, and people who become members are more likely to be noticed and helped than anonymous citizens of the community. (3) People's felt needs are not usually their ultimate needs, but are symptomatic of their ultimate needs. Faithful ministry engages both the needs people are conscious of and their underlying needs. (4) "Social lepers" need the classical gospel in addition to relevant ministries. In Luke 5, the leper says, "Lord . . . you can make me clean." Why did he believe a leper could approach Jesus? Other religious leaders were not, for lepers, approachable. Why did he believe that Jesus would touch him? No one else would. Why did he believe Jesus had a power to cleanse leprosy and make people whole? Why did he address Jesus as "Lord"—a theologically loaded title even that early in the messianic movement? The circumstantial evidence is clear: He had heard the early stories about what God was doing in the ministry of Jesus. He had heard some early claims about Jesus' identity. He was responding to the great news that was circulating.

The church, in response to social leprosy, has a threefold mission:

1. To be a *prophetic* church—working in season and out toward reform of those institutions, laws, customs, and habits that afflict people with closed doors, powerlessness, and low self-esteem.

2. To be a *serving* church—finding the colonies of lonely, dispossessed, lost, powerless losers, afflicted inwardly with low self-esteem, some committing slow self-destruction.

3. To be a *communicating* church—sharing the message and possibility of grace, reconciliation, and new life.

What might a church's "marketing approach" look like? Richland, Washington, is a small city with high population turnover. Pastor Joe Harding and other leaders of Central United Protestant Church observed, as families moved in one summer, that family moves are times of grief for teenagers, complicated by the difficulty of breaking into an established social scene in their new high schools. One fall, Central Church launched a new youth group for teenagers. They helped them work through their grief, and the group met some of their social needs. From that point on the group participated in writing their own agenda, with strong ownership in their program. The group remained together throughout their high school experience. The church now starts, each fall, a new group for new teenagers in town. By now, Pastor Harding has welcomed many of them into the church as first-generation believers, and has married some of them and baptized their babies.

Sunrise United Methodist Church in Colorado Springs, Colorado, is a growing first-generation congregation responding within a unique setting. In addition to its distinctly spiritual ministries, the church has engaged the felt needs of unchurched people through a range of human services—from aerobics classes to marriage enrichment and self-esteem workshops. Senior minister Ed Beck, once captain of a University of Kentucky national champion basketball team, does outreach to the faculty and student body of the nearby Air Force Academy and to athletes at the U.S. Olympic training center.

Aldersgate United Methodist Church of Wilmington, Delaware, identified a significant number of handicapped children in their ministry area, generally neglected by the community institutions. The church decided to "throw a party" one night each month for these children. They publicized it widely and personally invited many children, and eighty showed up for the first party. Church leaders noticed parents standing around during the party, and began a parallel program on parenting handicapped children—which met in several groups during the parties. Many of these families are now discipled.

When a church begins with people's felt needs and conscious struggles, it finds responsive people and comes to reflect the marketing orientation, which "holds that the main task of the organization is to determine the needs, wants, and interests of target markets and to adapt the organization to delivering satisfactions that preserve or enhance the consumer's and society's well-being" (Kotler, 1982, p. 23).

Steps in a Marketing Strategy

Much can be known today about marketing for churches that goes beyond the scope of this illustrative chapter, but we can outline four essential steps.

1. Gather information about the needs and wants of a target population, that is, a distinct group of people the church feels called to serve and reach. Three methods are generally productive: (a) *Interviewing* members of the target population or leaders and experts who work with them or possess information about them. Here the church wants data about the population, and also information on what is already being done to help them. (b) *Observing* the population, in ways that are unobtrusive. (c) *Reading* relevant literature, which is imperative. The following method can produce an astonishing array of articles in one day. An aggressive team of three or four people "attack" the nearest large library. They track down all the promising articles on, say, deaf children, suggested by an inexpensive computer search or from recent issues of the *Reader's Guide to Periodical Literature*. They photocopy the dozen or so

most helpful articles, put them in a binder, and leave several hours later with enough information to make an informed beginning.

2. Design ministries that might help the target population. Where at all possible, involve members of the target population in the planning. They will provide needed data, perceive possible mistakes, help determine which of the possible ministries would be most effective, and provide bridges to many other members of the target population. In any situation in which the target population or its key stakeholders can be included in the planning and executing of the ministry, there are no good reasons for "doing it for them."

3. Communicate the offer of ministry to the targeted groups. Be intentionally redundant, using personal invitations and appropriate community media.

4. Present the program, ministry, or service with the best management, execution, and human relations possible, and with evangelical follow-through. The bridge to the church from a mother's day out program, a low-budget clothing shop, or a marriage counseling center is not automatically perceived and crossed by the people being served. The church must often befriend them and invite them to respond. As one of many examples of the maxim that "you cannot not communicate," if church people do not befriend and invite them, it will communicate to them (whether or not the church intends it, whether or not the church is aware) that the church does not want them. Lyle Schaller once wrote a memorable prescription for a church becoming involved in "special ministries" ("Seven Characteristics of Growing Churches," *Church Administration,* October 1975, p. 8):

Regardless of the nature or content of this specialty in ministry, in the growing churches it has five common characteristics. It (1) is person-centered, (2) intentionally includes an evangelistic dimension,

(3) provides opportunity for members to be directly and personally involved in ministry to people outside the church, (4) offers opportunities for members to express themselves through expression of their creative skills (by contrast much of what is asked of volunteers in the rest of the church program places a comparatively high premium on competence in verbal skills), and (5) helps clarify the identity, role, and self-image of that church both to members and nonmembers throughout the community.

Effective marketing is essential to the growth of Robert Schuller's Garden Grove Community Church in Southern California. Schuller is a marketing genius, and in *Your Church Has Real Possibilities* he details how a church might get started. He believes that "the secret of success is to find a need and fill it." A church discovers unmet needs by surveying its community, door to door. "No two communities are alike, and you have to find out where people are hurting in your community" (p. 4). The church should call on the targeted neighborhood or population door to door for two weeks.

Listen to what the unchurched are saying and you will find out where they are hurting, where they are frightened, where they are worried. Take careful notes. Keep a daily diary detailing your calls . . . .
After two weeks you will know what kind of a church program you have to design to meet the needs of these people in your community . . . . You will even discover what kind of staff members should be added to your church. (pp. 81-82)

Case Studies in Compassionate Marketing

Some "world class" churches have remarkably varied ministries to people with needs. In the 1960s, the West London Methodist Mission, under Donald Soper's leadership, had institutionalized the following ministries:

Kingsway Crèche—for children
St. Luke's House—for alcoholic men
Stirling Court and Argyll House—"second stage houses"
    for alcoholic men
St. Mary's House—for alcoholic women
Grove House—for unmarried expectant mothers

Alfred Hartley House—for elderly women

Emerson Bainbridge House—residence for young people

Fellowship House—residence for young people

Hopedine—for unmarried mothers and their babies

Katherine Price Hughes Hostel—for girls in need of care and supervision

WLM Clothing Store—for those with little money

Today, the staff and laity also minister in other special needs that are not so clearly institutionalized, such as prison ministries, job placement, and work among prostitutes, drug addicts, and men newly released from prison.

Alan Walker expanded the work of the Wesley Central Mission in Sydney, Australia, after an apprenticeship with Soper in London. Today, the church's letterhead reports that the church

conducts an extensive program of Christian compassion through the mid-city: Wesley Centre, a hostel for the intellectually disabled; fourteen children's homes; a lodge for homeless people; a private hospital; a sheltered workshop; three farms and a refuge for alcoholic rehabilitation; a lodge for teenagers; three retirement villages and five aged care hostels; two nursing homes and a large hospital specializing in rehabilitative and terminal care; Do Care home visitation service; Wesley Central Mission Textiles and Recycling Industries; Wesley Home Care maintenance service; Wesley Film Productions; Life Line, Youth Line, Credit Line, and Ethnic Line telephone services; and Vision Valley, a conference center.

Wesley Central Mission's diverse agenda has been maintained and expanded by Gordon Moyes, Walker's successor, and a staff of more than one thousand. Moyes has added a national weekly television and radio ministry, and is referred to as "the Australian Schuller"! The church's various centers feature fifty-five worship services a week. Such churches as the West London Methodist Mission and Sydney's Wesley Central Mission illustrate what is possible, but ministries to needs are best understood one at a time.

First United Methodist Church of San Diego, California, features "Up from Grief" group meetings every Wednesday night. The ministry began in the mid-1970s, following a tragic airplane crash involving a dozen persons, who were suddenly and painfully left behind. The group experience opens people to the ultimate questions of death and the meaning of life. The groups have served as a port of entry into faith and the church for many people, and all of the Wednesday night group leaders are "graduates" of the program.

In the 1970s, the Friends Church of Southern California planted churches in communities of young couples with small children. In a strategy developed by John Wimber, leaders would focus on a neighborhood or a cluster of neighborhoods known to have many newly arrived young couples. Leaders did door-to-door surveys, first asking, "When you leave your home, where do you go most often?" Typical responses were a supermarket, laundromat, city park, or library. The surveyors then asked them to identify which supermarket, laundromat, and so forth, and recorded the places most often visited. Third, callers asked, "What kinds of particular problems, struggles, or frustrations do you experience as a young family—that you would like some help with?" Answers varied, but two problems mentioned often were "potty training" and "communication in marriage."

The Friends then rented a site, perhaps a meeting room at the library, and offered a potty training seminar—one evening a week for six weeks, with nursery available. They advertised the seminar on posters, at the very supermarkets, laundromats, and other places most frequented. All the parents who had reported potty training as a problem in the survey received a personal invitation. The Friends sometimes held several series of the same seminar to meet demand. The Friends then sponsored a seminar on communication in marriage, with similar publicity and results.

The Friends recruited, from the women who had participated in one or both of the seminars, a staff for a Vacation Bible School for children the forthcoming summer. Where all three projects succeeded, the Friends started a new congregation—with many of the couples as charter members. Every congregation planted with this strategy has thrived, most with an active membership of seven hundred or more within two or three years.

Leaders of St. Paul United Methodist Church in Abilene, Texas, noticed that no church in the city was using contemporary art, or engaging the city's art community. The church established a gallery in its building for the display of good local artistic expression, including photography and folk art. Under the direction of a volunteer fine arts coordinator, the church hosts and promotes an art show each month, as well as other occasional events. More than one thousand persons often visit one of their art shows. The church has realized three "spin-offs." First, many visitors to an art exhibit become familiar with the building and the church, and are more likely to visit the worship service or respond to an invitation. Second, the program has engaged a number of people in the art subculture. Third, some of the artists are now using their gifts to communicate Christian themes.

Early in the twelve years that Kenneth Chafin served South Main Baptist Church in Houston, Texas, leaders discovered in the 1970 census that more than 400,000 single adults lived in Houston. They also discovered that no visible congregation was reaching singles in significant numbers.

The church began a Friday evening seminar for singles, and advertised it on the entertainment page of the Houston newspapers. The seminar ran for four consecutive Friday evenings, and soon the series had to be repeated eight to ten times a year, each series attracting one hundred or more singles, 90 percent of whom had never before been to South Main Church. Some participants were widowed, and some never married, but a majority had experienced the agony of divorce. The church, having decided that "divorce is not the unforgivable sin," supported the program strongly. Chafin spent the last decade of his ministry there preaching to more than six hundred singles each Sunday, whose port of entry into the church and faith had been the Friday evening seminar.

In his book *Is There a Family in the House?* Chafin reports that singles come to the seminars asking staggering questions like, What do you do when all you want to do is die, after two years? Typically, however, the seminar's insights and the support of the group and church make a difference. Chafin shares a representative case:

Such a girl came to us looking years older than her age. She sat on the back row of the seminar on "Beginning Again" and cried all the way through it. Before coming to us, she had already tried all the other places in town to lose her loneliness. But now she was lonelier than ever. I think we must have been her last desperate effort to find help. Talking with her at the recess, I could tell by her defensiveness that she was afraid to relax with us for fear she would be used.

By the fourth week she had found a few friends and had begun to relax. She became involved in a support group which specialized in helping each other through rough times. Though her [earlier] experiences with the church had left her suspicious, she finally joined a class of seventy-five who were her age and involved in a Sunday morning study. I watched her over more than a year's time. It was like watching a flower open to the sunshine as she responded to the love and support she was receiving.

One day she stopped me as I was going into the building and said, "I don't know if you realized what kind of shape I was in when I came to that first seminar, but I was at the bottom in every way. I may have looked alive but on the inside I was dead to any feeling. What my divorce hadn't done to me I did to myself after the divorce. I know you've been interested in me so I thought you'd like to know. I'm beginning to feel alive again on the inside. And on my good days I even think maybe God has a future for me."

In recent years Harold Bales, pastor of First United Methodist Church of Charlotte, North Carolina, observed increasing numbers of street people in downtown Charlotte. The church developed an effective ministry to these people that involved a lunch program, job referral, a clothing shop, counseling, an uptown day shelter, and a storefront indigenous worship service on Sunday mornings. This "alternative congregation" has grown admirably, a number of street people have become disciples, and many are now working as volunteers in this ministry and reaching out to their peers.

Bales has consistently interpreted this as a compassionate ministry to "the outcasts and untouchables of our society." In his church newsletter he featured a poem recently written by one of these persons who found care and hope at the uptown day shelter:

If you're down and out and hate to show your face,
Well, this must be the place.
If you've lived on the streets and felt a lot of defeats,
This must be the place.
If you feel ashamed to tell people your name,
Well, man, this must be the place.

Let God help us all here, as we think of all those dear, who
    have enough and won't share, those who could and won't,
    because they don't care!
Well man, this must be the place.
For comfort from others in the same shoes as yours, get
    indoors out of bad weather.
Man, come to this place.

Korean churches probably approach ministry to target populations as imaginatively as anyone in the world. For instance, their interdenominational Christian Broadcasting System broadcasts weekly half-hour radio programs to many targeted groups, including taxi and bus drivers, homemakers, the elderly, children, teenagers, sick persons, handicapped persons, farmers, fishermen, and workers.

Seoul's Namsam Methodist Church, pastored by Byoung Hoon Kang, has reached great numbers of North Koreans who fled south during and after the Korean War. The North Koreans now living in Seoul have a distinctive history, a slightly different culture and dialect, and their own set of problems—isolation from family in North Korea, fear of Communism, and more.

Kwang Lim ("Burning Bush") Methodist Church, in Seoul, has grown in fourteen years from 4,000 members to 18,000 members, and may be the largest Methodist church in the world. Kwang Lim's senior pastor, Sun Do Kim, attributes much of their growth to their caring for people where they hurt. Their extensive pastoral care, mixed with worship, prayer, preaching, and some 1,200 geographically based house groups, is offered for "healing wounded hearts." Eleven pastors, nineteen Bible women, and many laypeople visit in homes each day.

In April 1985, when in Seoul as a speaker for the Centennial of Protestant Christianity in Korea, I asked pastors at a reception, "What inspires you and keeps you alive in the work of Christ?" One pastor reported the work of an elderly woman's group in his church: "This large group of sixty women meet one afternoon per week and make things to sell for mission. They provide support for a Korean missionary couple serving in Japan." I agreed that was impressive, and the pastor said, "That's not all. They all lost their husbands to the Japanese in World War II. Across our section of Seoul, there were hundreds of them growing old and bitter. My predecessor decided the church must find as many of them as possible, and show them the faith-power that frees people to love their enemies."

"Indigenizing" the Church's Ministries

A teenager became a follower of Christ in a thirty-year-old "second church" in, let us say, a town in Texas. Within several months the fellow, now a high school senior, reported to his pastor a persistent sense of being "called to the ministry." The pastor observed his growth with immense pleasure. The young man was sensitive, encouraged others, was articulate, studied the Scriptures, and spoke with transparent conviction in youth fellowship meetings. The pastor discerned the boy's "gifts and graces" for ministry, and even the "fruits"— his sister, mom and dad, and two high school buddies had become involved. The pastor decided the teenager's call should be announced; the young man would preach for the Sunday evening vesper service on Student Recognition Sunday.

That evening, so many people showed up that the service was moved from the chapel to the sanctuary. The people, whose church had never produced a "preministerial student," were genuinely interested. The young man's maiden voyage in the pulpit was not a model of homiletical art. His discourse was disjointed, his text was more a pretext, and his conclusion was abrupt. Still, the people were moved as they observed the signs of his growth in their midst. The Spirit visited that evening. Several teenagers, and others, came to pray at the altar.

Leaders of the Men's Fellowship, knowing the boy's limited economic circumstances, decided to help put him through college and seminary. They did this by sponsoring pancake suppers every fall and spring for seven years. The church's members and friends consumed a lot of pancakes! The young man also worked part-time those years.

After seven years, they arranged for him to return and preach on Sunday. They recalled the Happening in the vesper service seven years earlier, an event they had embellished in their memories. Now, in his return engagement, following an unsingable hymn that the people "had not even known was in the hymnal," he stood in the pulpit wearing a "clerical collar," read from a "pericope" in "Deutero Isaiah," and then proceeded to "exegete" the pericope and indulge in "hermeneutical interpretation." The sanctuary was a sea of puzzled faces and fidgety bodies. The young preacher missed his hometown people *in toto.* After the service the people stood around confused, having developed a distaste for pancakes. They groped for an explanation. Why, after expecting so much, had they experienced (and even understood) so little? Like any frustrated group, they seized the first plausible explanation: "The seminary corrupted him!"

He had not been corrupted, but the seminary had neglected one important facet of his preparation: While it had taught him to exegete a text, it had not taught him to "exegete" the context into which the text's meaning must be communicated. It had neglected to prepare him to become, for the rest of his life, a cross-cultural communicator of the Christian faith and heritage to his own people.

All education, including theological education, alienates folks who have experienced it from those who have not. We all recall the physician whose "explanation," in medical jargon, left us understanding the cause of our fever no more than before. We recall being frustrated while assembling a Christmas toy, attempting to follow an engineer's instructions written in Martian code. Such alienation may come quite early; we have all known a sophomore whose flaunting of his new knowledge and vocabulary alienated his blue-collar dad. Spending several years in the company of any branch of the Academy re-enculturates a student. She or he acquires the customs, ideas, tools, language, habits, tastes, assumptions, and style of that academic subculture, and it happens most to students who take their education most seriously. Every student learns to "say it the faculty's way," at least for exams and papers.

Theological education adds one peculiarity to this natural syndrome: The theological academy assumes its customs, jargon, taste, aesthetics, and style are superior to those of the members of Shiloh Church, and the theological academy (implicitly) licenses the rookie minister to shape up the Shiloh people and raise them culturally, by revising the liturgy to fit the seminary's model, and by having the people sing the right hymns and learn to pronounce the names of Augustine and Barth correctly. If the people are not educable, they are not OK! The Shiloh folks thus experience their new pastor as an elitist, or a snob, engaging in cultural imperialism. They usually lack the assertiveness to resolve the problem, so they vote with their bodies—by absentee ballot. The young pastor misreads the feedback, and quickly concludes their pew is vacant because his sermons are "prophetic" or because the neighboring pastor is "sheep stealing." It takes about two frustrating pastorates to get over this piece of one's education.

Ironically, this same young pastor would have adhered to a different script if he had been a cross-cultural missionary to people of another nation and language. His good sense would have instructed him to learn Aymara his first months in the high Andes, and as he formed a church he would not force-feed Gothic architecture, or pipe organs, or Elizabethan English, because he would know that to be effective, his mission work must be expressed in *indigenous* cultural forms. A people's culture is the incarnate medium of God's revelation to them.

Our young pastor, however, has not yet seen the need to adapt his work to people of a different subculture within his own general culture and who speak (more or less) his own national language. To compound the problem, some of his "church pillars" at Shiloh may be following the style and jargon of their doctrinal tradition, or denominational bureaucracy, or nineteenth-century revivalism, or pop psychology, or some TV evangelist. Longtime members may realize no more than their pastor the need to adapt the church's ministries to the culture of undiscipled people.

North America today is a vast mission field (*see* Parvin, 1985). The church's mission now faces, on this continent, more than 170 million secular undiscipled persons. Though they pledge allegiance to one nation, under God, and though half of them register a "religious preference" in surveys, they live their lives and make their decisions as pagans. North America is also an increasingly complex mission field. Twelve percent of our people are black (African, Caribbean, Jamaican, et al.). Six percent (and growing) are Hispanic (Cuban, Mexican, Puerto Rican, Latino, et al.). Many Native Americans live across much of the continent. Increasing waves of Asians (Koreans, Japanese, Filipinos, Thai, Vietnamese, Chinese, et al.) are immigrating to North America, the Asian population now projected to be ten million by the year 2000. Many regions and sections of the continent are bewildering mosaics of different peoples. South Florida, in addition to the Jewish and Cuban populations it is noted for, has seventy thousand French-speaking immigrants from Quebec, who are different from the region's seventy thousand Creole-French-speaking immigrants from Haiti.

Mind you, there are other complex mission fields on the globe. Small countries, from Guatemala to Nigeria to Papua New Guinea, necessitate ministry through a score or more languages. India, with its 700 million persons divided by sixteen major languages, with hundreds of distinct dialects, with its three thousand castes and forty million tribal people, and with its historically entrenched problems, is enough to challenge the most confident strategist. However, North America is now as diverse and complex as any mission field in the world, and the church is learning to see that North America, Europe, and Australia are no less mission fields than Africa, Asia, Latin America, and Oceania. In addition to the growing number of major language and culture groups, North America is a mosaic of numerous subcultures (preppy, yuppie, redneck, blue collar, silk stocking, et al.), classes, dialect groups, regional cultures, and interest groups.

The church, with other institutions, is learning that North America is *not* the "melting pot" of American mythology, but a mosaic of many genuine Americans or Canadians as fully intent on perpetuating their cultures and identities as are Anglo-Americans. Peter Wagner suggests the continent is a "stewpot" of many ethnic identities, each seasoning the others and being seasoned by them, while each retains its own substance (1979a, p. 51f.). Anglo-Americans no longer constitute a majority in North America, and non–Anglo-Americans are now the majority in at least twenty-five major American cities. North America is a continent requiring mission workers to adapt, because most of the people "out there" are not "like us."

Crash Course in Missionary Anthropology

There are, we are told, about thirty thousand distinct "societies" on the earth, each with its own culture. What is "culture"? It isn't going to the opera and eating caviar. Anthropologists, with some variation, define culture as *the integrated system of learned ideas, behavior patterns, and products characteristic of a society.* Let's look at that and illustrate it piece-meal, because knowledge of the cultural "soils" in which we would plant or spread Christ's church is imperative.

A culture has hundreds of its own learned patterns of behavior, commonly known as customs. Our customs make life manageable by making automatic how we go about most things, such as how we eat, sleep, acquire a mate, bury our dead, dress for work, settle a dispute, find a dwelling, greet a friend, deal with an in-law, or with an outlaw! For example, Anglo-Americans greet an acquaintance with a handshake, a friend with a hearty handshake, but Latin Americans characteristically embrace one another, Frenchmen brush one another's cheeks, and some South American tribesmen spit on one another's chests! Each society assumes "our" way is "natural" and their way is "strange." Understandably, South American tribesmen wonder why an Anglo man and woman sometimes greet each other by "sucking mouths"!

Each culture has its own ideas, which anthropologists categorize as values, attitudes, and beliefs. *Values* are our culturally defined assumptions about what is good or bad.

Anglos generally value profit, but some other societies do not. Anglos value "getting ahead," but other societies value "being one of the group,"—in Japan, "the nail that sticks out gets hammered." Socially, most Anglos like to be with their friends, but the people of many societies most enjoy their families or clans. A people's *attitudes* are the collection of what they, in common, are for or against. Anglo-Americans like baseball but not bullfighting. Spaniards like bullfighting, but they regard baseball as "boring," and English cricket as "baseball in a coma." A people's *beliefs* are the collection of what they, in common, assume to be true or false. Americans, "know" that a sickness is caused by a germ, but many tribesmen "know" the sickness is caused by an "evil spirit," and Melanesian tribesmen "know" the sickness is caused by some broken relationship.

Every society also invents and uses its own characteristic "products"—including tools, technologies, art forms, artifacts, ceremonies, rituals, and so on. Anglo-Americans characteristically eat with a knife and fork, but Australians put a sharp edge on one side of a fork and get by with one "splade." Koreans eat with chopsticks. Many tribespeople think nothing beats human hands for efficient eating, but Asian Indians eat with the right hand only. (In both cases they recommend the hand as an eating tool because "you always have it with you," and "you know who used it last"!) Even *when* people eat is subject to a culture's norm; many Africans eat once a day—in the evening—but Scandinavians eat six times a day, and Melanesians have no specified time to eat or number of daily meals—they eat when they are hungry. And *what* a people defines as worth eating may vary so widely from the food acceptable to another people that nausea is induced. We readily notice, in travel, a myriad of cultural differences in dwellings, art, music, dance, clothing, and so on.

But these obvious differences among peoples are not the important ones. The important differences are found in the world views of cultures, that is, the way they see the world, how they prioritize their values, and how they integrate the pieces of their culture. Anthropologists tell us that all of a society's common customs, values, attitudes, beliefs, and products are integrated into this world view, a "mental map" of the world, how it works, and how to cope in it. Furthermore, most of the people of every society operate out of "naive realism," assuming that their mental map of the world is right and is the way things are. A culture's mental map of the world is learned: We begin learning it in infancy. We learn it by watching others, by reward and punishment, and especially through our culture's language. There was a time when "our" way and world view were all we knew, and therefore it is natural that each people assume their way correct.

Why does a society develop a "culture"? To reduce decision making in daily life, to increase life's predictability, to cope in some way with humanity's basic needs—physical, safety, belonging, esteem, self-actualization, understanding, and aesthetic. Every culture develops some integrated system of customs, ideas, and products to meet these needs. One culture may succeed more effectively or obviously than another in fulfilling a need, which is why cultures sometimes change; but every culture is, by definition, successful enough to cope reasonably well, or its society would die out.

Human Experience Across Cultures

Cultures differ, and the people of each culture think "the way we do things" is "natural." When people of two cultures come into contact, or work together, the experience can be amusing, confusing, frustrating, or conflictive. Anthropologist E. T. Hall's *The Silent Language* showed, for instance, how varying assumptions about "social space" can cause confusion. Latin Americans normally stand closer to persons in social conversation than do Anglo-Americans. In a social exchange between two unaware persons, one Latin and one North American, this subtle difference can affect the relationship and their perception of each other. The Latin keeps stepping closer to achieve the "normal" distance for conversation, subconsciously wondering why the Anglo is so "distant." The Anglo keeps backing up to achieve "normal" social distance, subconsciously wondering why the Latin is so "pushy." Hall observed a lengthy conversation between a

Latin American ambassador and a U.S. ambassador, in which the Latin succeeded incrementally in backing the Anglo virtually across the entire ballroom.

Such "culture jolts" are often experienced when persons of two cultures work together. In international governmental and business relations, we are told that one side has more of an advantage when it understands the other party's culture than when it does not—as U.S. politicians have discovered in dealing with the Russians and U.S. businessmen with the Japanese.

Toward an Indigenous Strategy

This helps one to understand why the gospel's ambassador is called to adapt to the cultural forms of the target population. All of "us" have received the gospel "wrapped" in the clothing of our particular culture, and thus to us the faith spread. But when we too closely identify the gospel treasure with the earthen vessels in which we received it, its communication to people of other cultures or subcultures is frustrated. Our task is to "rewrap" the gospel in the clothing of their culture, to convey it in a vessel that will transport the gospel's meaning to them. The communicator wants to remove any "false stumbling blocks" between the target population and the gospel. The strategist uses their forms and language to express it in ways "natural" to them. McGavran observes that, through an indigenous strategy, "Natural witness by the whole membership becomes possible. The *naturalness* of Christian life and worship, witness and learning, is what tells. 'Unconscious' witness is perhaps the most potent element in growing churches." Indeed, he suggests, "There is *no defense* against this natural witness so characteristic of indigenous churches" (McGavran, 1980, pp. 380-81, emphasis added).

The recent history of Christianity in China illustrates McGavran's observation. In 1949, there were perhaps two or three million Christians in China. Then came Communism, the Cultural Revolution, and (most thought) the virtual decimation of Christianity in China. But in the 1980s a different picture has unfolded—of a church with no clergy, no Westerners, and driven underground and reformed into lay-led house churches. In the 1950s this modified form of "Christianity with a Chinese face" began spreading. By 1985, China's Bishop Ting was estimating the existence of one million house churches in China, and between ten and fifteen million Christians. The principle of indigenousness helps explain the growth of the church throughout the Third World. McGavran would add that "indigenous church principles are just as useful in Texas as in Tanzania and should be taken seriously by all students of church growth" (McGavran, 1980, p. 373).

The principle of Christian advocates and servants adapting to the culture of the target population has ancient precedents. Our Lord "emptied himself" and adapted to the culture of Galilean Jews. He spoke folk Aramaic, assured his people that he had not come to destroy their culture but to fulfill it, and the common people heard him gladly. Although Paul assured the Corinthian house churches of his absolute fidelity to the message of "Jesus Christ and him crucified" (I Cor. 2:2), he explained that the means of enabling this message's effective communication is the interpreter's willingness to "become all things to all men, that I might by all means save some" (I Cor. 9:22, see 9:15-23). The early church's biggest "shoot-out" (Acts 15) was between Paul and Peter over the issue of whether Gentile converts had to become like Jews culturally (Peter's position), or whether they could remain culturally Gentile and still be Christians (Paul's position). Paul's team won. The whole New Testament was written in *koine* Greek—the language of the common people, not of the academy—and various books of the New Testament, including the four Gospels, exemplify strategic adaptation to the original target audiences.

My colleague, anthropologist Darrell Whiteman, laments that, "Unfortunately, the lesson learned at the Jerusalem Council (Acts 15) has had to be relearned in nearly every era of the Church's history." When we understand the power of culture in shaping the way we think and live it is not surprising that in cross-cultural ministry "we" have expected "them" to become like us in order to follow Christ. Yet the enduring lesson of Acts 15 reminds us that such is not the Christian, or the effective, strategy.

We have noted that John Wesley rediscovered this principle, and developed indigenous field preaching, an indigenous hymnody, tracts and pamphlets, and plain language, identification with the people, and indigenous lay leadership to communicate and advance early Methodism. He even innovated in the area of indigenous church architecture.

Late in the nineteenth century and early in the twentieth, missionary thinkers like Nevius, Allen, and Hodges began reflecting more systematically on these strategic matters, but the strong advancement of a practical theory of indigenousness awaited the rise of cultural anthropology as a discipline, and its offshoot, missionary anthropology. Today, some perennial questions are addressed more effectively than ever before.

One question, of great strategic importance, is, How much must one adapt one's witness and ministry to the target audience's culture to be effective? Ralph Winter's now classic model helps us to understand that the amount of adaptation required (and the degree of difficulty involved) largely depends on the "cultural distance" between the mission worker and the target population. By this model, we communicate the gospel to people at an "E 1," an "E 2," or an "E 3" cultural distance and level of difficulty ("E" being the symbol for Evangelism). I have defined these distances from my own vantage point, as follows:

> E 1 evangelism involves the communication of the gospel to people generally of my own language and culture. I am a citizen of the U.S., though I logged two years vocationally in England, and five years in Texas! There are millions of persons in the U.S. and Canada, and even in Great Britain, Australia, and South Africa, with whom I can communicate more or less "naturally," though E 1 connotes that some distance or barrier is involved, namely the "stained-glass barrier" between Christians and non-Christians. To communicate, we must adapt enough to begin where they are, but

learning a different language and getting oriented to a different system of customs, ideas, and products in order to adapt is not part of this challenge.

E 2 evangelism involves communication of the gospel to people of a different language and culture, but still of the same cultural "family." For me, communication with the Hispanic ("Mestizo") peoples of Bolivia is at an E 2 level of difficulty. Their language and culture are significantly different from mine, but they are still a "Western" culture and so, in addition to my "phrase book Spanish," they pick up meanings in many similar words, from body language, facial expressions, and some inflections, and we may even experience some overlap in what we find amusing. Mind you, the jump between E 1 and E 2 is a very large one, even larger than the next jump in difficulty, from E 2 to E 3.

E 3 evangelism involves outreach to a people of a very different language and culture, from a different cultural family. For me, communication with Aymara Indians in Bolivia is an E 3 experience. Their culture is of a "non-Western" family of cultures, so they pick up few of my words and gain little meaning from my gestures and body language—although some facial expressions may be universal. But effective communication with them depends largely on the skills of my interpreter.

Communication at the E 1 level of difficulty is obviously more manageable than E 2 or E 3, and many more people are able to do it. It *is* easier to relate, communicate with, and evangelize one's cultural near neighbors. When a church is growing mightily, the faith is typically spreading among people who are only at an E 1 distance from one another. If, say, Juanita Romero is not a disciple but is open and searching, Theresa Escamilla (who is at an E 1 cultural distance from Juanita) is, presumably, in a better position to communicate the faith meaningfully than is Mary Murphy (who is at an E 2 distance).

But that fact raises Ralph Winter's major point: At least 2.5 billion persons (representing some 16,750 distinct societies, speaking more than 5,200 distinct languages or dialects) have no indigenous church, no cultural near-neighbors from whom they are likely to be exposed to an indigenized (and therefore understandable) expression of the faith. These are the "unreached peoples" of the earth, and many of them are the "hidden peoples"—whom Christians (with the resources to reach them) do not usually think about, or know about.

The unreached peoples constitute the reason why the age of cross-cultural missions is not over (even though the era of European colonialism *is* nearly dead). What is more, although many of these hidden peoples reside in the "Two-Thirds World," many are residing in the cities of North America and Europe as well. In Lexington, Kentucky, the First Alliance Church started a Chinese-speaking congregation, reaching a people that most of Lexington's other churches did not know were present.

So in Church Growth theory, to begin new Christian movement within the ranks of the target population, we begin at the cultural distance we have to. But the sooner indigenous converts become the primary communicators, the sooner the movement will spread rapidly. This strategic understanding in no way negates, however, what the Holy Spirit is able to achieve through cross-cultural witnessing across great cultural distances. In the fall of 1984, I preached several times, through a lay interpreter, in tribal language black churches in South Africa. In one service, twenty-two persons accepted the invitation to follow Christ through his church. God blessed and multiplied our efforts that Sunday morning, yet his primary strategy for discipling this people does not call for continual droves of people from a Western culture, like me, but rather for indigenous communicators.

The Problem of "Nominal" Christians

The early use of the E 1, E 2, and E 3 distinctions in Church Growth literature left some outreach tasks unclear. For instance, if our objectives for people in Church Growth are that they (1) become followers of Christ and (2) become incorporated into the body of Christ, what is our relationship to people who have met the second objective (they are involved members of a church) but not the first (they are not yet followers of Christ)? There are perhaps 700 million nominal Christians in the world, most of them second-, third-, or fourth-generation church members, who are baptized and may attend worship, but have not yet experienced God's grace and become followers of his Christ. Four policies are suggested for this population.

First, Church Growth people have designated this as E 0 evangelism, meaning there are no cultural barriers between "us" and "them," not even "the stained-glass barrier." They are already members, favorably disposed to the faith, and open to the church's ministries, though many have accepted a diluted version of the faith—which has "immunized" them against a full dose. Receptivity, however, ebbs and flows in marginally churched people also, and the sensitive church will recognize its opportunities.

Second, wherever such people are still in the church, this should be perceived as an opportunity we may not have forever. Canon Bryan Green reminds us that, for decades, the Church of England had millions of undiscipled persons who were nevertheless semi-active members of parish churches, but that the church missed its opportunity and has thus suffered decline in membership. Green does not recommend that other churches repeat the mistake.

Third, many nominal Christians are "awakened" and searching, and John Wesley would advocate welcoming (and retaining) awakened people into "class" and "society" membership, whether or not they are yet disciples. The step into the fellowship is a distinct and necessary step in the *"ordo salutis,"* and almost all justified Christians were first members of the church, or at least involved in its life and fellowship, prior to experiencing Christ's acceptance and becoming his followers. Wesley commends the smaller redemptive cells as the form of church in which the faith is most likely "caught." We see, in the cases of awakened people who were not yoked into class and society and later fell asleep, this need to involve awakened people in the fellowship. Wesley also observed a high percentage of awakened people who were retained in class and society who, in God's good time, experienced their justification and knew they belonged to Christ.

Fourth, Church Growth research into what churches are really doing in evangelistic ministry tells us that many churches are too preoccupied with their own inactive nominal members. Perhaps 90 percent of what takes place in a typical church's "evangelism" program is directed toward its own inactive members. There are several problems with giving first priority to "our own inactives":

1. They are usually perceived as having been "insincere" when they joined, though there is little data to confirm that assumption. The data suggests they were just as sincere when they joined as were our active people, but, after joining, they never felt like they belonged, were part of the fellowship, and would be missed if not there. Typically, they stayed away awhile, weren't missed, and became inactives. The cause of the inactive-members problem is more often located in the church's program for new member assimilation than the original motives of the inactive member. Another major cause of dropping out is unresolved conflict with other members or the pastor.

2. Because of that prior experience of unresolved conflict, or feeling rejected, or not really included, it is not easy for "their" church to win them back. Your inactive members, now, may be the most resistant population to your church in your ministry area. As noted, it is not wise to expend the most outreach energy on resistant people, but on receptive people.

3. In many cases, it is possible for another church to attract their involvement. Upon reflection, we would rather a person be an active Lutheran (or Baptist or Catholic) than an inactive Methodist (or Presbyterian or Episcopalian). Members of ministerial associations might exchange photocopies of their inactive rolls and tackle the problem more effectively in this way.

4. Interview your inactive members. Get their story; find out what went wrong and why they felt rejected or "spit out of the system." Then you can change the congregation's approach in ways that will reduce the chances of the *de facto* exclusion of other new members. Sometimes, when inactive members are visited by a nonjudgmental caring listener from the church who lets them "talk it out," they will work through their resentments and try involvement again. Will their experience be better the second time around?

5. We are beginning to challenge the assumption behind E 1 evangelism that there are no important cultural differences between a church's active members and its inactive and marginal members. If the assumption is generally valid, it has countless exceptions. My own observation and interview research discovers many people who do not quite fit the majority culture of a church, but joined it for one reason or another, and these (now) marginal or inactive members *do* have important culture-related differences from the active membership, differences that are felt by them to be important. Subcultural barriers may partly explain the marginal and inactive status of millions of nominal church members. But we lack, to date, the research to show how extensive this cause is, since "new member insincerity" and "inadequate assimilation ministries" have been assumed to be the only causes. Churches who develop more indigenous ministries and groups for the subcultures they reach will effectively include many members who vary slightly in culture from most of the members.

Reaching Across Subcultural Barriers

We have found that Winter's E 1, E 2, E 3 model left one fundamental matter unclear: whether the communicator's distance from some people is E 1 or E 2. As an Anglo-American, am I at an E 1 or an E 2 distance from my supermarket's Polish-American butcher? What about the black fellow I met at the gym (who doubled my bench press)? Or the Appalachian woman who is now my barber? An early confusion surfaced in Church Growth literature when some writers suggested that communicators perceive people of a different culture and language as an E 2 challenge, but other writers regarded another subculture (within the communicator's general culture and language) as E 2. For us lesser mortals who do not "pick up languages easily," the difference between communicating to another subculture and communicating to another culture is immense. So, in *Global Church Growth,* I published a refinement, and McGavran built upon it to suggest that "instead of two sharp classes, E 1 and E 2, there are several kinds of E 1, gradually shading off toward E 2" (McGavran, 1980, p. 68). In other words, the E 1, E 2, E 3 model awakens us to the cross-cultural challenges in world evangelization better than it awakens us to the more subtle subcultural challenges within E 1 evangelism. A new awareness to communicating between subcultures may prove to be the major discovery of the 1980s, and it is now being emphasized throughout the "helping professions." Gerard Egan even maintains that "culture . . . affects all interactions, even between those of identical twins. Since no two individuals grow up having exactly the same set of beliefs, values, and norms, even interactions between identical twins have a cross-cultural dimension to them. A working knowledge of the power of culture is a relatively new tool for helpers" (Egan, 1986, p. 12).

So I expanded the E 1 category into E 1-A, E 1-B, E 1-C, and E 1-D (do bear with me, or skip for now this technical discussion):

Evangelizing at an E 1-A level of difficulty engages those people of the communicator's own culture and subculture who are his or her own intimates—relatives, colleagues, and close friends. With these he has many natural links. These links are "the bridges of God" discussed in chapter 4.

Evangelizing at an E 1-B level engages people very much like the communicator, but they do not yet know, or spontaneously trust, one another. In customs, socioeconomic class, education, vocation, needs, lifestyles, backgrounds, aesthetic preferences, and in many values, attitudes, and beliefs, they have much in common. The communicator can therefore speak and relate quite naturally to them. Little or no cultural adaptation is required, though initial rapport will have to be established. The communicator may find usable the same evangelistic method and motivational appeal that engaged him or her. The communicator's testimony may be appropriate and potent in E 1-B communicating.

E 1-C engages people of the evangelizer's culture but of a different subculture. As the evangelizer and (especially) the recipient sense their differences in customs, lifestyles, education, vocabulary, class, aesthetics, or whatever, these differences are experienced as subcultural barriers. The recipient, perhaps subconsciously, asks, Why don't I feel comfortable with her? What did he mean by that word? Why is she talking to me? What is his axe to grind? In short, it is harder for the recipient to trust and respond to a communicator of a different subculture than to one of his own, and it is a more rigorous task for the communicator, requiring adaptation . . .

E 1-D engages people of a hyphenated subculture. In North America, for instance, we have mentioned the rich cultural mosaic that makes up Canada and the U.S. In their cultural identities, many people are Afro-Americans, or Mexican-Americans, Polish-Americans, Cuban-Americans, Korean-Americans, and so forth. Their group consciousness is "hyphenated." Most of these people become "American" enough to make a living, bargain for a car, "psych-out" the Anglos, and otherwise cope, but they intentionally retain their former cultural identity, believe it to be beautiful, intermarry, pass their identity on to their children, and socially interact chiefly with "their own people."

E 1-D is not as difficult as E 2, because they have experienced enough re-enculturation to provide some points of contact with, say, the Anglo-American evangelizer. But the "how" of reaching them is more complex than E 1-C. It will require initial probing, interviewing, and experimenting to discover felt needs, points of contact, and the appropriate responses that will make communication possible. As in the case of many target populations, interviewing those who have become first generation Christians will uncover the approaches that would engage others like them. (*See* McGavran, 1980, pp. 63-72, some modification included here.)

This expanded culture-typology of evangelism calls to mind two implications: First, a particular congregation may primarily be able to expand its ranks by discipling men and women who are only at an E 1-A or E 1-B cultural distance from most of the members and leaders. It can attract a few people from an E 1-C distance, a very few from E 1-D, and even fewer from E 2 or E 3. The winning of some of these latter may be done by starting indigenous groups within the congregation or an alternative indigenous worshiping congregation within the church. In most communities, however, these people will be discipled in great numbers only by starting new congregations in separate spots that are indigenous to them in language, culture, liturgical style, and leadership. Many churches should hedge their bets both ways—attracting all who will come, and planting daughter congregations for those they would like to welcome into their own ranks but who are unresponsive to the mother congregation.

Second, in order to begin a Christian movement among an unreached target population, the evangelizers should begin outreach at whatever cultural distance will engage the most receptive among the undiscipled. The sooner the new converts within each piece of the mosaic evangelize their own people, the more rapidly the faith will spread. A contagious Christian movement among a people will develop when church members of a given subculture reach across existing social networks.

Guidelines for Indigenizing

How do you go about indigenizing a church's ministry, witness, and worship to fit a people's culture? This is a crucial question, because the culture of another people is the medium of God's incarnational revelation to them. Darrell Whiteman says that "the Incarnation is the model; indigenization is the method." But what is indigenization? Mission's effectiveness depends on this, and eight guidelines should help Christians find their way in this thick jungle.

First, to acquire a genuine *sensitivity* to cultural factors and to people of other cultures is to win half the battle. This generally requires a Cultural Anthropology 101 experience in basic anthropological knowledge, an immersion experience in another culture or subculture, a willingness to take some risks and not take oneself too seriously, some feedback on how one is communicating in the target culture, a collegial relationship with one or two "confederates" in the other culture, and reflection on what is learned.

Second, consciously work to *identify* with the people, to understand and empathize with their customs, their feelings, their felt needs, their "mental map" of the world. Enter into some genuine friendships, and spend leisure time with these friends. People will ask certain subconscious questions about the cross-cultural communicator, like, Is she with us? Is he for us? Is she almost one of us? Complete identification may never take place. Anthropologist William Reyburn once martialed a lifetime of anthropological knowledge and research of Quechua Indians into an experiment: to pass himself off as a Quechua Indian. In village after village he failed to pull it off, though he looked something like them and knew more about their customs, dress, and other matters than any other Westerner. Asking how they could tell, he was told by one chief, "You did not have a Quechua mother!" Cross-cultural identification is never complete, for some things are learned only in early enculturation, but partial identification seems to be usable by the Holy Spirit, who makes up the difference.

169

Third, the use of their *language* is usually essential, preferably their dialect or even their "heart language." Mission history does not record many achievements where the language the missionaries used was not the recipient population's language. In McGavran's early years as a missionary educator in India, he followed the mission station's established practice of teaching the Bible to Hindi-speaking boys in English, out of the mission station's objectives to teach both Scripture and English. They learned a lot of English and a little Scripture, and not many became Christians. One year, McGavran taught them Scripture using a Hindi translation. Now the Word took on life and was perceived as God's word for them. They learned more Scripture, and many more became Christians. What does this imply about, say, an English-speaking Presbyterian church in Akron, Ohio? If it is counterproductive to minister to Hindi-speaking boys in English, it is also counterproductive to minister to Appalachian tire company workers in Princeton English, or to insist they sing "aesthetically preferable" hymns. In the subcultures of the various cultures, the Word must be spread in the language and cultural forms of the subculture if it is to become flesh.

Fourth, use a *style* of clothing, church architecture, hymnody, worship setting, and liturgy to which the subculture can resonate. There are people within any target population who can tell you what "fits" them and what does not, what they like and do not, what is within their comfort zone and what is not, what they can respond to and cannot.

Fifth, employ appropriate *responses*. The kind of pulpit evangelistic invitation that fit, and gathered harvests in, frontier nineteenth-century camp meetings may not fit and gather harvests today in Beverly Hills, or Berkeley, or Brooklyn, or Baton Rouge, or in Bristol, Buenos Aires, Bangkok, or Bombay. Peter Wagner has illustrated the crucial importance of indigenous harvesting methods: If one entered a wheat field ripe for harvest, but attempted to gather the harvest with a cornpicker, one would not effectively gather the harvest and would even destroy much of it. To discover the best method or methods, observe those methods God is already blessing amongst these people. If there are no harvests yet being gathered, interview self-aware members of the target population, asking, How do your people work through and act on some new possibility for your lives? What do you do that fixes a decision, makes it memorable, and helps it stick?

Sixth, employ an indigenous style of *leadership*. There is no one best style of leadership, because one style of leadership may fit the experiences, development, and expectations of one people and not that of another. For instance, a pastor may effectively run a "blue collar" church like a factory foreman—fairly authoritarian but in real contact with the people. On the other hand, if that same pastor imports that style of leadership into a church of managerial and professional types, they will help him reenact the Exodus!

Seventh, recruit and develop *indigenous leaders*. It frequently matters what people make up the church's leadership. Thousands of small churches across North America are perceived to be dominated by one family or clan, with other people invited to help pay the bills and watch the Williams clan perform and make decisions. Also, it frequently matters what people make up the *visible* leadership, especially in a "transitional church" experiencing population turnover in its ministry area. A Church Growth strategy for such a church would:

1. Perceive the change in the community as an opportunity rather than a problem, a new community taking shape rather than an old community dying.

2. Quickly move to attract and disciple the most receptive of the new population.

3. Quickly develop and elevate some of the new people into positions of visible leadership, so that others who visit will not feel they are invited guests "in somebody else's church."

4. Make culturally appropriate changes in the image, style, hymnody, and liturgy of the church—involving these new leaders in the choices.

5. Reach out across the social networks of the people you have already received, and invite relatives and friends to become involved. Reach out across their networks, and so on.

6. Start new ministries that engage the felt needs of the target population.

Eighth, encourage indigenous *theologizing*. Darrell Whiteman reminds me that theological reflection emerges, typically, as the church in a given culture seeks biblical answers to important questions raised by that culture. For example, in a country (like Japan) with a tradition of ancestor veneration, the church should develop a theology that addresses the issue of how Christians are to think of their ancestors. Again, in a country (like the U.S.) with a visibly affluent life-style, the church should teach how to live as a Christian in the midst of affluence. Because cultures are different, their respective societies face a somewhat different set of life questions, which should be addressed by the church of that culture (which is a different dynamic than spoon feeding the set of answers developed by another church in a culture with a different set of problems). Churches with an indigenous theology communicate the meaning of the gospel and spread the life of faith in their society more effectively than churches depending on an imported theology.

Test Questions

Having attempted to "indigenize" ministry to fit a people's culture—that they may understand the gospel's meaning —how do we appraise our efforts? The following "test questions" are suggested, to be discussed with members of the target population:

1. What have we changed since we started taking "culture" seriously?

2. Does the target population feel "comfortable" in the church, in its worship and ministries? (The comfort, in social situations, of all peoples matters to them more than it "ought to"!)

3. Do we seem to identify with one another and with what is going on?

4. Does the target population feel ownership in the mission and priorities of the church?

5. Do the people feel that the forms of worship, leadership, and church life are natural to them?

6. Is the meaning of the gospel getting through? Is revelation taking place in their hearts? Are there some new disciples?

7. Are outreach and invitation to involvement taking place across their natural social networks?

On "Homogeneous Units" and Church Growth

We are now in a position to discuss the "homogeneous unit" controversy in today's church—triggered by reactions to McGavran's generalization that "people like to become Christian without crossing racial, linguistic, or class barriers" (McGavran, 1980, p. 223). At one level, the statement is self-evidently valid. The clothing in which the gospel is wrapped effectively for one culture may not fit another, and most people of any culture identify with, feel comfortable with, and understand better people of their own culture more than those of another. In my teenage years in Miami, Florida, if the only Christians had been Gypsies, or Creole-speaking Haitians, or rich people in Miami Beach, I might not have become a Christian. Indeed, few people become Christian in a church where they are neither like the people in the church, nor aspire to be like them. Even objectively petty cultural factors that shouldn't be barriers sometimes are. A few Sundays ago, I heard a fellow from another region of my country preach, and—to my culturally conditioned ears—he missed every vowel in the sermon, as he heralded "saelvashun in Chriiist." His dialect was exasperating. I rejoiced, however, to see that others present were deeply engaged and moved as the Word was preached in their heart language. I have since asked a dozen persons (all Christians, all considering themselves "progressives" ethically and "inclusive" in their churchmanship) if there are any American-English dialects that annoy them. They have all concurred, and have given examples. McGavran is pointing out that most people experience similar language and cultural barriers, and they find it easier to respond when such cultural barriers are absent.

Most of us, however, are not able to look at this issue as objectively as McGavran, who was raised in India, spent his "first career" in India, and first discovered this principle in researching the church's growth within India's complex caste society. The American mainline Protestant conscience was imprinted in the 1960s. We struggled with racism in American society and others, and still continue that struggle for justice. What, then, can be said that will generate more light than heat?

It is crucial to understand that McGavran is concentrating on *culture,* focusing on the cultural factors that make a given person's response possible and more likely in the company of some people. The theory in no way supports any form of segregation or apartheid. This point is demonsrated by many black churches in North American cities today, in communities where the churched black people have experienced redemption and lift and are moving out to other neighborhoods. Other blacks are moving in, but blacks of a different subculture, and the black church experiences great difficulty reaching the new black people. Here, the barrier is obviously not racial, but cultural. Again, many "racially integrated" local churches are culturally homogeneous churches, that is, most of the people are similar in such cultural features as education, vocation, life-style, and interests; the basis of their homogeneity is cultural, not racial. McGavran has always considered the homogeneous unit theory a strategy for including all peoples in the church and for excluding no people. But what, more specifically, should be the church's policy and hope? I offer several suggestions:

First, the church universal is called to effectively include all peoples, but one reason we multiply churches is because no one local church can effectively minister to every people. Open to all people, of course; wanting all people, emphatically; but effective with all people, in no way. For instance, in metropolitan Chicago there are more than sixty major language populations. No one local church ministers to more than five or six language groups, and these churches are exceptional.

Second, in a world of practical trade-offs, some situations require homogeneous unit churches that sacrifice for now the ideal of a culturally inclusive church for the sake of, say, helping a disadvantaged people. The Christian movement has discovered in Peru, Ecuador, and Bolivia that you cannot for now combine Quechua people and Aymara people into the same congregation if you desire to develop the leadership of Aymara Christians, since the Quechuas (for longstanding reasons) tend to dominate the relationship and become the leaders. In North America, when several subcultures attend the same church, most of the leaders come from the subculture that is the most advantaged, is most educated, has the most experience in chairing meetings, and so forth. Of course, any homogeneous church is penultimate to the church that is to be, and while homogeneous churches seem to be more effective at bringing people like them into faith and church, heterogeneous churches more effectively model the kingdom of God and what the church is intended to be.

McGavran reports that there are countless situations, especially urban, in which "culturally conglomerate" churches not only model the Kingdom better but are also strategically better at reaching many people who do not yet follow Christ. In situations where we cannot predict whether a homogeneous church or a heterogeneous church can reach a people, perhaps the most faithful and effective policy is to give people options and trust that their sense and the Spirit will lead them to the best option.

175

Finally, in more and more situations it is possible to effectively offer people the conglomerate church, providing three prerequisites are met and maintained: (1) The leaders must be culturally aware, and must collaboratively devise indigenous ministries for the people of each involved culture. One proven model is the South Main Baptist Church in Houston, who hold services (and Sunday school classes) simultaneously in five languages—English, Korean, Spanish, Chinese, and Vietnamese. Some ethnic people, especially the young, who are more fluent in English, go to the English service, but all groups share many experiences and ministries. (2) The church needs to staff for the diversity it intends, and plan to fund their more diverse ministries. Heterogeneity requires more resources and staff than homogeneity, a price eminently worth paying, but best faced up front. (3) There will be conflict in growing churches involving several cultures. There is conflict in most churches anyway, including growing churches, but culture clashes will surface when two or more cultures work together and will be added to the other sources of conflict. Leaders need training in conflict management. Conflict is "natural" to all organizational life and to multicultural life and work, and is a kind of energy. When badly managed, however, that energy can fragment the organization and defeat its mission. When well managed, it can provide energy for great achievements, achievements in which the people may see proof of the presence and power of God.

One statement from above merits repetition: "Any homogeneous church is penultimate to the church that is to be, and while homogeneous churches seem to be more effective at bringing people like them into faith and church, heterogeneous churches more effectively model the kingdom of God and what the church is intended to be." There are, of course, other penultimate forms of the church as well. Churches that are not evangelizing the lost, or sending cross-cultural missionaries, or supporting peace and justice, or nurturing their members toward maturity in Christ, are examples. In truth, most of our congregations are penultimate forms of the church on several scores. But effective church leaders have learned to begin with churches as they are, rather than as they would like them to be. Likewise, McGavran would have us know the wisdom of beginning with the people of the earth as they are, rather than as we would like them to be.

Today, most of us feel drawn between two poles—the mandate for indigenous ministry to each people and the Kingdom ideal of the united new humanity. It is helpful to be reminded that each of the two poles has its legitimacy, the same person can affirm both, and the achievement of the first is a necessary step toward the second.

Wesley achieved this integration admirably and would commend it to us. Martin Schmidt, perhaps the greatest Wesley biographer, tells us (1973, pp. 173-78) that Wesley understood profoundly that there are differences of class and culture, and that one must take this as a fact of social reality without pretending its nonexistence and "without being filled with envy and jealousy or contempt." For Wesley, "Part of a sense of sobriety was a basic recognition of the fact that God's 'drawings from above' take different forms and that individual souls had to be guided in different ways."

And yet, in the Methodist societies, "High and low, rich and poor, rubbed shoulders with one another, and . . . a person of exceedingly low intellect, perhaps even mentally retarded, was assured of full respect" (Schmidt, 1973, p. 178). Indeed, Wesley believed that part of a Methodist society's genius and power "was the bringing together of unlike minds" (though the classes tended to be more homogeneous).

First United Methodist Church of Coral Gables, Florida, is currently moving from an historically "silk stocking" image toward outreach to many peoples in metropolitan Miami. They now broadcast, by radio, their Sunday morning worship service, by which people of several subcultures become involved in the church, and others—such as housebound people, nursing-home dwellers, and people who work on Sunday mornings—now constitute a "network congregation," who are prayed for and visited, who may join the church and give by mail to its ministries.

One day senior pastor Riley Short received a note of gratitude from a Robert Gibbon, who included a check. Several more notes and a generous check were received.

Short saw a Miami Beach address on the envelope and decided to make a pastoral call. His pursuit of the address led his car through a post-transitional section of Miami Beach and to a Hoagie Hut restaurant. Short asked, "Is there a Robert Gibbon here?"

The cashier replied, "Sure, he's the dishwasher. I'll get him."

Gibbon emerged, and Short greeted him with, "Robert Gibbon? I'm Riley Short, your pastor. I've come to see you." Gibbon embraced him, and eagerly introduced "my pastor, Riley Short" to the cashier, the manager, several waitresses, and several perplexed customers.

Short said, "Robert, we would love to have you join First Church."

Gibbon replied, "I'd like to, but I don't know when I could; I'm at work every Sunday before your service is over."

Short exclaimed: "No problem! I could receive you as a member right now, on this spot!"

Gibbon: "Let's do it!"

Short: "I declare Hoagie Hut restaurant an outpost campus for First United Methodist Church of Coral Gables, and these people now assembled are a congregation. Robert Gibbon, do you accept Jesus Christ as your Savior and Lord, and intend to follow him the rest of your life?"

"I do."

"Will you be loyal to the church, and uphold it by your prayers, your presence, your gifts, and your service?"

"I will."

"Robert Gibbon, in behalf of all God's people everywhere and of all time, I welcome you into the family of Christ."

They later found that Robert Gibbon could attend the church's early service and Sunday school, and still get to the restaurant in time to work. Gibbon is now a greeter for the 8:30 A.M. service. Not long ago, Bishop Earl Hunt came to preach, and Gibbon greeted him, "We are pleased to have you preach, Your Excellency."

They discovered that Gibbon could play the piano—and rather well. An international corporate lawyer, who teaches a Sunday school class for older people, told his class, "Our class needs a regular piano player," and when they agreed, he invited Gibbon to join "the team." Gibbon comes to the church every Sunday before 8:00 A.M. to practice the hymns they will sing. They say that Robert Gibbon smiles more now—since the class bought him a set of teeth, and since the church opened up opportunities for him to serve Christ's church through his gifts.

Meanwhile, Back in Texas

Several years passed, and the church in Texas invited the (fairly) young minister back to speak at a special service. Not that they were itching to endure another sermon like the last one. Their judicatory had organized a program for all its churches, and one piece of the program called for congregations to invite a minister to speak who had come out of their midst. Since this young man was the only minister they had produced, their options were limited.

He was now pastor of a promising Protestant church in a section of San Antonio, a predominantly Roman Catholic city. He had "bombed out" in his first pastorate. Attendance had declined steadily. The people had believed him conscientious, and they liked his wife, but they did not understand him; they sensed his agenda was different from theirs. Certain core leaders became frustrated and alienated, and they "negotiated" his move by a certain date. The young pastor was unable to indulge in the rationalization that the leaders were "unfaithful," because he had seen their faith and compassion on too many earlier occasions, and he didn't like to think his ministry there had corrupted them. He experienced great agony and wondered if indeed he were called to the ministry.

He asked to visit a more senior minister, in a neighboring church, who had been a missionary in Korea before taking his present church. After a lengthy conversation, this experienced colleague discerned what had happened, and asked, "Do you think of yourself as a missionary serving that church?"

"No, of course not, but my wife's brother is a missionary in India."

179

The senior minister replied, "You are a missionary too!" Knowing he had the young minister's attention, the senior minister chatted about the relevance of culture, even when one is serving people of one's own nationality. He talked about the importance of language, and leadership style, and music, and respect for customs, illustrating out of his experience in Korea and from his present thriving ministry. The young minister exclaimed "Aha!" as some of his frustrating experiences began to make sense. In the young man's remaining months in that region, the two men talked frequently, and they read and discussed books on anthropology, cross-cultural communication, and church growth. The young man was getting a "new and exciting act" together as he prepared to leave his first pastorate for the church in San Antonio.

On his last Sunday, the leaders approached him and said, "You've gotten a whale of a lot better since we mutually decided to change ministers. We hope our next minister is as good as you are becoming! Keep it up!"

As he and his wife drove their rented moving van to San Antonio, he shared with her how he was changing. He said, "I take 'culture' and people more seriously now. I'm not as quick to write them off. I'm not giving up anything I got at seminary—except some snobbery. Most important, I'm learning to find out where people are and begin there. And I'm learning to communicate the meaning of the church's gospel and tradition so that people can catch on!"

He made a good beginning at the church in San Antonio. He got to know the people, their background, their culture. He asked them about their dreams for their church and community, some of which made perfect sense, and he said, "Let's pull together and do them." After one year, some of these goals were visibly achieved, attendance had inched up consistently, the church knew where it was going, the spirit was up, and on Sunday they baptized an adult couple into the church as new believers. By now he had removed his clerical collar for good—not because of the occasional public confusion about his identity in that Catholic city, but because of occasional confusion about his wife's identity!

The Sunday back in his hometown was worth remembering, and celebrating. He spoke from Paul's text "I have become all things" and so on, and then shared the story of what he was learning—"that some might be saved." He spoke clearly and honestly, in ways they could understand. They heard the Word of God. They sensed the Spirit again. A young high school football player and a young woman studying at a community college were both in attendance. To their astonishment, each sensed a mysterious stirring within, and wondered, Am I being called to be a minister of the gospel?

C H A P T E R   8

Strategic Planning for a Church's Future

Planning has usually been crucial to the spread of the Christian faith. The movement's history is not without its sovereign providential surprises and its periods of apparently spontaneous expansion. The earliest church seems to have exploded across the Judean hills. Jonathan Edwards was surprised by the effects of his preaching, which triggered North America's first Great Awakening. But even those movements, which began without planning, were not sustained without planning, and effective prayerful planning is usually involved in the launch of an evangelical movement as well.

Pope Gregory's sixth-century sending of Augustine and forty other monks to the British Isles "to make angels of the people called Angles" involved sophisticated initial planning. Today's Bold Mission of the Southern Baptist Convention involves denominational planning at, perhaps, an unprecedented level of sophistication, though the planning of some Roman Catholic mission orders also excels. The work of the Lausanne Committee for World Evangelization has demonstrated how the reaching of an "unreached people group" requires research and planning. The history of many once-declining, now-growing churches reveals a season of dreaming, praying, and planning for the future during their pivotal period. The way forward for many churches involves an informed approach to planning.

The Scriptures counsel the people of God to plan. *The*

Living Bible's paraphrase of the book of Proverbs declares that "the wise man looks ahead. The fool attempts to fool himself and won't face facts" and, "A wise man thinks ahead; a fool doesn't, and even brags about it." So we should make plans—counting on God to direct us.

Effective planning in eighteenth-century Methodism made possible a growing network of classes, within societies, within circuits. The itineraries of the many preachers required planning, as did the nurturing of people, the training of leaders, and the spread of the movement. Wesley thought seriously about the future; he even projected several possible scenarios for the people called Methodists. Wesley especially focused on the movement's apostolic objective of "deepening and widening the work of God": he based all planning on that objective, and on the other driving values and doctrines of the movement.

The chief setting for planning Methodism's future was the annual conference of the preachers, and their planning was fairly collaborative from the beginning. Wesley convened the first one in 1744 for the purpose of asking his colleagues "to give me their advice concerning the best method of carrying on the work of God" (*Works*, Vol. 8, p. 312). Their first conferences were frustrating; owing to insufficient time, "Scarce anything has been searched to the bottom. To remedy this, let every conference last nine days . . . " (*Works*, Vol. 8, p. 299). Part of the conference was devoted to a rehearsal, with any needed clarification, of "what to teach," "how to teach," and "what to do." They then deliberated the future together. Wesley has been criticized for not leading "democratic" conferences in which things were determined by majority vote (*see* Ayling, 1979, pp. 175ff.), but the movement was held together by stronger glue than majority votes: (1) They affirmed common doctrines, objectives, and values, and (2) they met until their understanding of the way forward was unanimous. While the movement's objectives, doctrines, and driving values were givens, virtually every-thing else was negotiable (as Peters and Waterman, in chapter 12 of *In Search of Excellence,* have shown are characteristics of effective organizations). Wesley's usual refusal to control the conference's planning was especially apparent in the historic conference of 1775, when the conference responded to John Fletcher's challenge for more decisive steps toward the reformation of the Church of England. Though Wesley had a monumental stake in the discussion, he kept silent throughout (Schmidt, 1972, p. 121). Wesley believed strongly in the participation of the whole conference in planning their common work. There was a special power in all the preachers being yoked together in mutual ownership of unanimously supported plans. Once the conference had determined the major directions, the conference was then in position to make final the particular operational plans—such as projects, budgets, and the appointment of the preachers.

Francis Asbury built upon and extended Wesley's partici- patory model in the American conference. One example is in the way he moved into the fledgling denomination's top leadership. Though he had been appointed by Wesley to superintend the work in America, in the 1784 conference in Baltimore he sought (and gained, after open discussion) election to the position through his colleagues. That same conference discussed, and passed, a resolution retaining Wesley as spiritual leader of the movement.

Thus we see the importance of planning to evangelization, and we anticipate certain themes in informed planning, such as data, values, objectives, participation, ownership, and operational plans.

Why Rethink Our Planning?

Most churches do not yet perceive their need for more effective planning, because they already do a lot of it. They do, indeed, because most churches are beehives of programs and activities, and each program and activity is planned, usually in meetings, as the people nail down "who will do what by when?" When people regard themselves as "experi- enced" at something, it seldom occurs to them to learn to do it better, or differently.

Yet, despite all those plans, programs, and activities, most churches do not achieve much, and their people lack the satisfaction of being involved in significant achievement. The cause of this problem is suggested in a statement attributed to Hemingway: "Never mistake motion for action." About four-fifths of our churches are beehives of random (or inherited) motion, but not of action that will achieve something.

How do churches get this way? George Odiorne, a management guru, reports (1974) that organizations typically begin with a clear mission and goals, and they devise programs and activities to achieve the goals and fulfill the mission. But over time, the ends are forgotten and the programs and activities become ends in themselves. The people now focus on "the way we've always done things around here," the programs and activities become impotent and less meaningful, and the organization bogs down in "the activity trap."

The church that desires liberation from this trap (and a small host of other problems) needs a clear set of objectives. This is seen in the research-based conclusion of Richard Beckhard (see Burke, 1982, pp. 283-85), who understands the life of groups and organizations at four levels: (1) Objectives and Priorities; (2) Roles and Responsibilities; (3) Procedures and Processes; and (4) Interpersonal Relations and Behaviors. Beckhard's revolutionary insight involves the perception that an organization's problems are usually experienced at levels 2, 3, or 4, but are usually symptoms of an unrecognized problem rooted at a higher level. For instance, I consulted in a church that was a human relations quagmire. Almost everyone was angry at almost everyone. They lacked clarity and consensus in regard to the most elementary procedures and roles, such as who decides when to schedule a second worship service, or who banks the offering each week, and in what account. They had no clear mission as a congregation, and no clear objectives and priorities.

Virtually any church being used by the Lord of the Harvest has clear objectives, with plans for their achievement. This may be a universal law. I have observed no church experiencing sustained growth where there was not also an informed strategic plan being implemented and with widespread ownership. Although most churches have many plans, those plans are not at the service of a master plan, so the church stagnates and waffles, attempting to ride off in many directions at once. There is a line of questioning that a people must answer together before a stagnant or declining church can experience renaissance: If your church gets where it's going, where will it be? What will this church be like when it grows up? Describe this church as you intend it to be ten years from now. In the words of Galsworthy, "If you do not think about the future, you cannot have one." Robert Schuller states similarly, "If you fail to plan, you plan to fail." Historian Page Smith, a student of movements, tells us that "the leader with a system, however inadequate it may ultimately turn out to be, is at a vast advantage over a systemless rival, however brilliant."

I saw this truth operating in a community not long ago. My client church had a competent, devoted, and active membership, and a competent and credible pastor, but the church was experiencing slight decline in its membership strength—amidst a harvest! Down the street, another church was bursting at the seams and entering its fifth building program in six years. The second church's pastor and people were no more dedicated and competent than the first, but they had one advantage: Virtually all of their people, groups, and resources were being used in a concerted effort to achieve a few priorities. On the other hand, my client church had no consensus mission; some groups were pursuing their own objectives and agenda, others were engaged in mere activities, and overall apathy reigned. This large and serious truth is especially relevant to today's tens of thousands of apathetic churches: Bishop Ensley (1958, p. 51) paraphrases Toynbee as declaring that "apathy can be overcome only with enthusiasm and that enthusiasm can be aroused only by two things. One is the ideal that takes the imagination by storm. The other is a definite and intelligible plan for carrying the ideal into practice," of which eighteenth-century Methodism was a sterling model.

What Kind of Planning?

What kind of planning are we talking about? The kind reflected in one of Will Durant's more important conclusions from a life devoted to historical research: "The future never just happened. It was always created in the minds of men and women." I define *planning*, for our purposes in Church Growth, as *the mental creation of the future we intend*.

Notice that this definition embodies an aggressive and "interactive" stance to the church's relationship with the unfolding future. This contrasts with three other postures that organizations (including churches) sometimes take. In a *reactive* posture, leaders try to undo the present and return to a past state of affairs. In an *inactive* approach to the future, leaders take few risks and assume that any change would probably be worse than the present arrangement, so they work to preserve the status quo. In *preactive* planning, leaders adopt the philosophy emblazoned on Boston's 52-story Prudential building: "The future belongs to those who prepare for it." Preactive planners use present trends and their hunches to predict what the future will bring, and thereby prepare their organization for a secure place in that anticipated future. What used to be called "long-range planning" employed this philosophy. By contrast strategic planning takes an *interactive* approach to the future and believes that, although we will be impacted by a future that we cannot fully predict, we can also impact that future and help shape what it will be. Organizations with this bias work to design the future and the organization's contribution to it (*see* Ackoff, 1974).

Planning from an interactive stance involves two stages. In (1) *strategic planning*, the organization defines the future it intends and lays out the major stepping stones. It is analogous to planning a trip by determining (a) where you are now, (b) where you want to go, and (c) how you want to get there. (2) *Operational planning* takes up where strategic planning leaves off, addressing a multitude of specific questions (like preparing the car for the trip, how the trip will be paid for, where and what the family will eat, who will drive, arrangements for lodging on the way, and so forth) to be answered with "who will do what by when?"

Most churches do operational planning, and have many such plans behind their various programs and activities, but most churches neglect strategic planning. The problem is that operational plans only make sense when their various programs and activities contribute to the objectives of a larger strategic plan. In a large metropolitan regional church in a southern city, a chancel revision committee was formed when the new pastor saw that more room between altar and chancel rail was needed for serving communion. The committee extravagantly overshot their mandate, met for three months, and printed a document of a dozen pages with many recommendations, two of which were to move the pulpit to the side and raise the altar. Those two changes alone would have changed the congregation's approach to worship and would have taken the church in a different direction than it had, historically and with success, been taking. The proposals for change were not necessarily bad, but they presupposed major shifts in the church's philosophy and direction that had never been openly proposed or discussed. Some folks caught this in time and prevented the church from being hijacked.

A Strategic Planning Process

Planning is more important than plans. That is, while it is important that a church's trip into the future follow a map, it is crucial that the people, together, prayerfully define their future and the impact they intend. In this case, process is more important than product. To devise some "good plans" that then collect dust achieves nothing, but when people get their intentions clear and those intentions drive their decisions and their organization, great things are achieved. The steps in the prescribed process that follows are taken from many sources in Church Growth, management, and planning and have been observed or field-tested in enough churches to be proved feasible.

I. Church and Community Identification. A local church swims, carves out a future, and makes a redemptive contribution with an environment, which it may think of as the world, the denomination, or (especially) the community around it. A planning committee might begin by identifying what they will mutually understand their church's environment to be. The perception of many churches of what should constitute their environment, or field, is currently restricted by an inherited "parish" mentality; the field of opportunity was once understood to be all the people within walking distance of the church. Today, effective leaders think of a "ministry area," which is defined as all the people within reasonable driving distance from the church. This one step can extend significantly a leader's perception of the field of opportunity. Many people will drive twenty minutes or more to get to the church that understands them, meets their needs, and speaks their language.

Second, leaders should identify the essential type of church they are entrusted with, a typology based not so much on size, denomination, tradition, or the color of brick as (1) its location, (2) the people it reaches, and (3) their understanding of their community within the total community (*see* Anderson and Jones, 1978, ch. 3). For instance, it is widely observed that many persons do not neighbor much with their "neighbors," that is, geography no longer defines most people's social networks. A person, today, seems to neighbor on one of four bases:

1. Some people do their neighboring within their residential neighborhood.

2. Some people neighbor within a larger region of a city or community.

3. Some people are "cosmopolitan" citizens of the entire city.

4. Some people relate to a widespread "homogeneous" network of persons with whom they share the same language, background, handicap, or interest.

Within that framework, we speak of six types of churches widely identified in North America. A church's basic "type" is important to identify, because churches make mistakes in planning when their identity is not clear, just as a family may goof in not taking seriously their car's "type." Imagine trying to transport a family of five, Grandpa, the Irish setter, the luggage, and the baby's playpen in the family's compact car. Then imagine, after shifting all personnel and cargo to the van, they start out with only the gas money budgeted for the compact. Neither plan makes sense. The following typology will help a church's leaders identify what type of "car" they are driving.

1. *Downtown Old First Church* was the first church of that denomination in the city. Its founding generation included many of the city's pioneers and founding leaders. Typically, First Church helped start most of the other churches of that denomination throughout the city.

Located downtown, the church has the strategic advantage of being located on "neutral turf." In social perceptions, downtown "belongs" to everyone, so when someone visits First Church they do not feel they are entering someone else's turf. Partly for this reason, First Church probably attracts a more heterogeneous congregation than any other church.

Furthermore, First Church tends to attract cosmopolitans who think of the whole city as "their" community. The cosmopolitans, all over the city, are First Church's "market." It can win them more effectively than other types of churches, and some other types of churches will not be able to win many of them at all.

2. *The neighborhood church* is located in, and largely of, a residential neighborhood of a city or suburb. Sometimes it carries the neighborhood's name, as in Edgewood Presbyterian Church. Sometimes it is located adjacent to the neighborhood school.

The church's future is strongly tied to the neighborhood's future. Most of the people it reaches live in the neighborhood, or in an adjacent neighborhood, especially those whose neighboring pattern is with their neighbors. Or they once lived in the neighborhood, but moved out (and "up"), and they continue to worship in the old neighborhood. Their children will not, however, and those who still return are less likely to accept leadership posts, and those who do may not be sensitive to the community's changes and opportunities and may be emotionally committed to keeping the church "the way it has always been."

3. *The metropolitan regional church* is a visible church, located on the major traffic artery (or at the intersection of two main traffic arteries) in an identifiable region of the city. It may carry the region's popular name, as in Southland Christian Church or West End United Methodist Church. It attracts people from "this side of town," especially persons who think of that region as their community. The metropolitan regional church frequently grows to great institutional strength and strongly supports the wider mission of the denomination.

4. *The special purpose church* exists (get this!) for some special purpose. Unlike the other types, its location has little to do with its effectiveness. It engages persons of a particular language, background, handicap, emphasis, or cause—and if its mission is serious and its market exists, those folks will find it no matter the location. So, in North America today, we see a growing number of Korean churches, congregations for the deaf, charismatic churches, peace churches, and others.

5. *The town church* is located at the commercial core of a town with a metropolitan population of between, say, 500 and 20,000. It may be, particularly in smaller towns, the only church of its denomination. Similar in many ways to the downtown church, it is located in "everybody's territory" and can therefore attract people from a wide ministry area.

6. *An open country church* is located on a rural highway, or on some secondary road in open country. It serves the people who live in a sparsely settled rural area, or those who have moved to town and return to worship—but whose children will not return when they grow up.

Although most open-country churches are small-membership churches, limited membership strength is not necessary. Some open country churches have become quite large as they have expanded their vision, identified the many undiscipled persons in their ministry area, and devised programs and ministries to engage people's interests and needs. Many such churches have new opportunity as early retirees move to the countryside, and as others build homes in the country and commute on the new interstate highway to work in the city.

The opportunities for new strategic insight through such a typology are sweeping. Think, for instance, how many Downtown First Church leaders (whose church reaches cosmopolitans) could be liberated from self-flagellating feelings of guilt because "we are not reaching the people who live right around the church." Downtown First Church may never reach most of those folks, despite its good intentions, because many of those people are neighborhood people (although the downtown church could be the means of reaching them, by starting an urban neighborhood church —of, by, and for those people, with indigenous leadership, liturgy, and architecture).

Or, think how many neighborhood church leaders could avoid getting upset when members of a downtown or metropolitan regional church visit a family "in our neighborhood." In its neighboring and community patterns, that family may feel more at home in the downtown church than in the neighborhood church. Think how many churches would feel free to visit folks "within the shadow" of another church if they understood community today the way people do. Or, think how many declining neighborhood churches who missed the opportunity to change with their neighborhoods could have a second chance, by intentionally becoming a special purpose church.

Or think what a renaissance denominations could experience through planting as many metropolitan regional churches as possible. Those churches, as a type, tend to grow the most, prosper the most, and give the most money to the other causes of the denomination. They are often the denomination's wisest and most strategic investment. The new Presbyterian Church in America has devised a long-range strategy for reaching and serving the peoples of Atlanta. The first step involves the planting of fifteen to twenty metropolitan regional churches, each at some intersection of Greater Atlanta's Perimeter Road and some other major thoroughfare. These Perimeter Presbyterian churches will grow and prosper, making possible, well before the turn of the century, an extensive inner city ministry.

II. Situation Analysis. Now the church gathers data about the church and the community, in an effort to discern the main facts and trends that will help inform the planning process. Many leaders are tempted to skip this step, assuming they already know the facts relevant to planning. This assumption is usually wrong. Unless we systematically identify and gather the facts we need, our impressions are at the mercy of whatever random facts have seized our attention. In any case, the whole planning group needs a consensus understanding of the situation. To be motivated to acquire this understanding requires confidence in facts, which comes from knowing that planning (and outcomes) cannot be much better than the facts that inform the planning. As computer folks say, "Garbage in, garbage out."

Data gathered about the church should include the usual data and graphs about the membership's gender, age spread, education, and socioeconomic-vocational status, especially of members received in the last two years. Furthermore, each of those new members should be interviewed to discover what in the church attracted them, what needs they came with, what ministries engaged them, what experiences they have found significant, and their ideas about how other people like them could be reached. Many times, such practical research will reveal the ways forward and will show strengths upon which to build.

Determine, also, the church's membership strength trends. Scholars who have studied movements tell us that the effectiveness of any movement correlates with a movement's membership strength and whether that strength is increasing or decreasing. "Membership strength" does not refer to the people who are nominally attached to the movement or think it "jolly good." It refers to the number of persons who are substantially grounded in its core convictions and values, whose identity is attached to the movement, who attend its meetings and activities, and who devote time, money, or energy to help the movement's objectives to be achieved.

Through appropriate increases in its membership strength, a movement attains the "critical mass" needed to become more effective in achieving its social objectives. I once observed a denomination's regional body discovering the reverse of this principle. In 1960, the churches of United Methodism's Detroit district reported about 50,000 members. By 1970, they had declined to about 25,000. By 1980, they were down to less than 13,000 members, and they discovered they no longer had clout in metropolitan Detroit. They were regarded as an inconsequential minority, to whom the captains of industry, the press, and the politicians no longer listened. The Methodist leaders became interested in Church Growth.

How do you determine, at least approximately, the membership strength of a congregation? One way is to gather, for the preceding ten years (as possible), five pieces of data:

1. Active resident membership at year's end. This is *not* the most important indicator of membership strength. For instance, a "600-member church" with an average of 300 in worship attendance is probably in a stronger position than a "700-member church" with 200 in average attendance, although the number of people attached to the church and open to its ministries is not insignificant.

2. Average worship attendance for the year. This may be the most important indicator of membership strength; it is certainly the most immediate. It tells you how people are voting with their bodies, but does not

tell you what they are voting for (or against). Interviews tell you that. If something magnificent (or catastrophic) occurs in the life history of a congregation, the event will be reflected much sooner in the worship attendance than in the membership roll.

3. Average church school attendance for the year. Define this in whatever way is useful and fits with practice, but be consistent—so that you are measuring the same thing from year to year. The number of people who gather weekly in some group for fellowship and study is obviously important, and the number of adults who do so may be the most important indicator of membership strength of all.

4. Number of persons regularly involved in the church's ministry of the laity to persons, inside or outside the church's physical facilities. Define this in accord with your philosophy of ministry, but do not count persons performing mere ecclesiastical chores. A church that has increased by 50 percent the members involved in ministry to persons—scouting, meals-on-wheels, teaching Sunday school, finding the lost through visitation, or whatever—is obviously in a much stronger position than a church whose lay ministering forces have been cut in the same period of time.

5. Number received as new Christians for the year. Define this according to your tradition (confirmands, baptisms, professions of faith, etc.). This factor indicates the seriousness and effectiveness of the church's apostolic agenda.

Churches are encouraged to weigh these indicators in a way that makes this formula consistent with their philosophy of ministry and emphasis. For instance, in my church I might multiply the average worship attendance by two and the professions of faith by ten, before adding the five (philosophically adjusted) indicators to determine an overall indicator of the church's strengths and trends.

As a climax, project those trends out over the next ten years, showing (approximately) where this church will be by then—if we continue as we have been and nothing dramatic intervenes. Then ask if that is where we want to be in ten years. Planning theorists call this difference (between where you will be if nothing changes, and where you want to be) the *planning gap*. That gap helps planners discover how much change must occur, and to infer the magnitude of plans, resources, and so forth, that will be required to achieve their objectives.

The situation analysis also involves discovering important trends in the ministry area, and facts such as the number of functionally undiscipled people, the most receptive groups, their image of the church, the growth (and causes) of colleague churches in the area, and the experience and projections of other helping institutions such as schools and hospitals. In many cases, the church's planning committee will not have to gather most of this data. It can exploit the most recent census data. It can employ, for a session, the expertise of someone who knows the shape and trends of the community the best, such as a city manager, a county planning commission chairperson, a newspaper editor, or a school system superintendent.

In all of this research, the object is only to find out WOTS UP! WOTS UP is an acronym for the Weaknesses, Opportunities, Threats, and Strengths that will Underly your Planning. That is, you want to identify the weaknesses and (especially) the strengths in the church, and you want to identify the threats and (especially) the opportunities in the community. That is all. In other words your goal is not to amass piles of data you will never use. Your goal is intelligence, eight or ten pages at most of streamlined well-written material, emphasizing what the whole committee most needs to have in mind as it plans. By the way, devote no more than one season to this part of the process (and preferably less), lest you bog down in "the paralysis of analysis."

III. The Strategic Framework. This step may not be logically necessary in the strategic planning process, but it is psychologically necessary. It prepares the planning group for planning. It prepares people in the whole organization to "own" and carry out the resulting plans. It provides the climate and the perspective for seeing the church, its opportunities, and what it can achieve. The step consists of two tasks to be worked on simultaneously.

The first task is to identify the areas in which the local church is not experiencing the key outcomes it desires, but could achieve. Here, the leaders collaborate with many others to make a long list of possibilities, and gradually narrow the list to four, five, or six priorities in which many persons in the church have a stake. For instance, a church might identify ministry to unchurched young families, involvement in world mission, ministry to deaf people, Sunday worship attendance, and the church's physical facilities as their priorities.

The second task, pursued simultaneously, is to identify the church's stakeholders, defined as all those persons who have a personal interest in what the church becomes and achieves. This roster would obviously include the church's other significant leaders, its active members, its inactive members, and probably other potential (or actual) stakeholders such as its judicatory executive, family members of active members and of children in the Sunday school, community leaders, leaders of other service institutions, and target groups in the community whom the church feels called to reach and serve.

As committee members fan out to survey the church's stakeholders, in groups where possible, in personal interviews where necessary, they ask questions like: Our church's planning committee wants to get our church's act together for the future. What should our church be achieving that is not happening now? What are our church's strong opportunities to serve and reach people? What one area of concern occurs to you where we need better outcomes? This collaborative approach to planning becomes synergistic, generating more good ideas than the committee could brainstorm by itself. It reveals possible priorities for which there may already be a consensus, or at least widespread interest. Later, as the committee has collaborated with these stakeholders at several stages of the planning and as the emerging plans reflect the concern and wisdom of the whole people of God, the chances of the plan's being effectively implemented are greatly increased. The planning committee's goal is not to construct the "best" possible plan, but rather the best plan that will be implemented. Planning is not an end, but a means to new achievement.

IV. The Mission Statement. The committee may work for a month or six weeks on the first three steps. They usually work on them simultaneously, or alternate between pieces of one task and another, but they typically give undistracted effort to composing a mission statement. It is the most important single step, since the last four steps depend on it and flow from it. A committee may generate dozens of possibilities, from stakeholders and from its own thinking. As the committee narrows down a statement, it may write many drafts before it refines a version that shines and is ready to fly.

The mission statement is important also because, if well written and serious, it declares the major direction the church intends to take, the supreme purpose for which the church will exist. A strong mission statement becomes the driving force of the organization, shaping decisions (including budget priorities) and holding the church on course. Strategic planning scholars tell us that effective mission statements are (1) Brief—no more than one hundred words, and preferably much less; (2) Simple; (3) General; and (4) Energizing. Some scholars add that the mission statement should answer three questions: (1) What? (2) For whom? (3) How?

Sometimes, effective mission statements take the form of mottoes or slogans and are used in public relations, as in Dupont's "Better things for better living through chemistry," but a mission statement must be more than merely a motto or slogan. If it does not drive the organization's budget, decisions, and activities, it isn't a real mission statement. And its primary audience is internal. It shapes and drives the decisions, priorities, and activities of the organization's people. It expresses the organization's supreme and unnegotiable values. Note, for instance, the five principles of Mars (the candy people):

1. Quality—The consumer is our boss, quality is our work, and value for money is our goal.

2. Responsibility—As individuals, we demand total responsibility from ourselves; as associates, we support the responsibilities of others.

3. Mutuality—A mutual benefit is a shared benefit; a shared benefit will endure.

4. Efficiency—We use resources to the fullest, waste nothing, and do only what we can do best.

5. Freedom—We need freedom to shape our future; we need profit to remain free.

Examples of church mission statements abound. The Spring Hill Avenue United Methodist Church in Mobile, Alabama, declares their mission to be "Sharing and Caring to Meet Hurts and Hopes." First Christian Church of Ashland, Kentucky, reports their mission as "Reaching Up to God, Reaching Out to People." The Disciples Church in Eminence, Kentucky, see their mission as "Communicating God's Love to Meet People's Needs Through the Power of the Holy Spirit." In any mere collection of statements, one does not know whether they drive their church, or are mere window dressing, unless one investigates. It is probably important that a church *not* simply import a mission statement from another church. Even though, ultimately, the reasons for a church's existence are revealed and not negotiable, a church still needs to devise a local indigenous expression of its mission.

Shepherd of the Valley Lutheran Church, a metropolitan regional church in a sector of greater Phoenix, has grown over the last decade into one of the strongest Lutheran churches in North America. They attribute much of their growth to the mission statement they developed prior to becoming a contagious movement in Phoenix: "To Know Him and to Make Him Known." It quickly became their driving force. Senior pastor Dick Hamlin reports that they periodically appraise every program, activity, and group in the church for whether each clearly serves the purpose "to know him" or the purpose "to make him known," and they eliminate any program that does not, and will not, do either. Hamlin has perceived that "it is good to start things, but we must learn to stop things," to free up precious resources (time, money, facilities, human resources, etc.) for the priorities of the congregation's mission. This mission statement that has served them so well is not etched in granite, however. When I last talked to Hamlin they were struggling to add another piece: to "Know One Another." But they had not yet incorporated this theme into a larger statement that did not sacrifice the rhetorical power of the original statement.

Their mission statement, strong as it is, does not meet all the criteria (above) for an effective mission statement. As I observed the church and interviewed there, I sensed that a "textbook" version of their mission statement might read: "Shepherd of the Valley Lutheran Church is a people-affirming metropolitan regional church, committed to knowing him and making him known through compassion, worship, group life, and ministries of the laity." But I like their cogent version better. In a world of trade-offs, one should eagerly sacrifice some things for the sake of clarity and energy.

V. Objectives and Goals. Clear objectives, defined as "the outcomes we want and intend to achieve," are crucial to the effectiveness of any organization, including a church. An effective organization of people is managed through clear, salient objectives. A steady fix on objectives prevents a church from drifting off course, or slipping into the activity trap, and helps the church not only to "do things right" (efficiency) but to "do the right things" (effectiveness). The objectives flow from the mission statement, are consistent with it, and begin to turn strategic planning from a general into a specific process.

Two objectives are clearly implied in Shepherd of the Valley Lutheran Church's mission: (1) to know him, and (2) to make him known. The church sometimes operates with those objectives in mind, particularly in its critique of existing programs and resource deployment, but when actually organizing programs and ministries, the church operates with four specific objectives for people. The church proposes, through ministry, to help people:

1. Get Right!
2. Grow Right!
3. Go Right!
4. Glow Right!

201

In the "Get Right" objective, they want people to get right with God, that is, to understand and realize their justification by grace through faith and be reconciled to God. In the "Grow Right" objective, they want people to become informed by Scripture and theology. In the "Go Right" objective, they plan evangelistic outreach through the people. In the "Glow Right" objective, they form Christians who are contagious and have depth.

In strategic planning, each objective should be matched with one or more goals. Setting goals for which the people hold themselves accountable is a pivotal variable in Church Growth. A decade ago, Peter Wagner led week-long Church Growth seminars in Latin America, giving participants the opportunity to complete their training by setting growth goals for their church for the next year and agreeing to report a year later. Some set goals, some did not, but all had the same training. One year later, those who had not set goals were only slightly more likely to have experienced church growth, but those who set goals were much more likely to have experienced church growth. (Admittedly, reaching our numerical goals may not be intrinsically important, but our objectives are. The goals help us to see whether we are reaching our objectives, and our willingness to set goals indicates the seriousness of our objectives, our willingness to own them, and our willingness to manage the church by objectives.)

How do you tell whether goals are good goals or not? Lyle Schaller commends the acronym SAM, which helps us remember that useful goals are specific, attainable, and measurable. I modify the second criterion to read "Attainable with Stretch." It serves no noble purpose to merely set goals that perpetuate mediocre achievement. Good goals are a means to greater achievement, so they should "stretch" us, but not excessively. This is not the time for extravagant, unlimited wish listing. Our purpose in this exercise is to gain new direction and forward momentum for the church, so it is better that we exceed reasonable goals than that we try hard but fall short of unreasonable ones. Picture, hypothetically, two churches, each about 200 members strong, each studying Church Growth and about to set growth goals for the next year. Bethel Church sets a goal to grow by 20 in the next year, Shiloh Church by 100. In that year, Bethel grows by 25 and Shiloh by 40. Shiloh Church has, presumably, achieved greater outreach, but Bethel Church is in a much better position, psychologically, to face a new future bravely. The Bethel people now say, "Wow, we exceeded last year's goal. We are on a roll. Let's tackle something bigger," but the Shiloh folks say, "Goal setting? That didn't work. We didn't reach half of last year's goal. Let's not do that any more."

Other criteria for useful goals are sometimes advocated in planning literature. The people's *ownership* of the goals is important for their implementation, hence the wisdom of the collaborative approach, which involves stakeholders early and throughout the planning process. Other writers say that if the goal-related responsibilities and milestones are not *scheduled,* then the group does not have a goal it intends to achieve. Again, planners might set goals in realms where the church has some control. For instance, undiscipled people in the community have control over whether they respond to the church's invitation, so a church might select a goal for how many people they will invite—a factor they control—but might not select a goal for how many people will join—a factor the church does not control.

Shepherd of the Valley Lutheran Church sets quite long-term goals. When I was there, in winter 1984, they had 547 persons regularly involved in some ministry of the laity. They are working to have 900 involved by 1990, and 2,000 by the year 2000! Dick Hamlin is confident in the future of their mission, and of Christianity's mission. What is the source of this apostolic confidence? He confesses, "I peeked. I read the end of the Book!"

VI. Strategies. A strategy is the broad action you will take to move toward achieving your objective. Typically, an informed planning group will generate a fairly large number of possible strategies, from which they will choose the most expedient to run with, or perhaps the best several strategies, which they will execute in tandem. The previous five chapters of this book have delineated five mega-strategies that growing churches characteristically follow, in some modified form, to achieve their growth and service objectives:

1. Identifying and reaching receptive people.

2. Reaching out across the social networks of believers.

3. Multiplying units as recruiting groups and ports of entry.

4. Ministering to the felt needs of people.

5. Building culturally indigenous forms of ministry.

Many other strategies may be identified in particular churches and communities, and undoubtably, further research will uncover additional universal principles.

An abstraction that may not be apparent is the synergistic way the strategies interact when several are in place. One example may suffice. A secular couple's marriage was in great jeopardy. They realized they did not have the answers or their act together, and became open (1) to "some glue, from somewhere, that could hold this thing together." One summer evening, a friendly couple in their neighborhood (2) invited them to visit a new couples' Sunday school class (3) that the neighborhood Baptist church was starting. The lesson was, "Covenants: Making and Keeping Them," (4) and one couple shared how the power of Christ in their lives enabled them to forgive each other, stop hurting each other, and reconcile their marriage. The new couple stayed for worship and were astonished that there was a church that seemed to understand people like them, that spoke their language, and even sang songs they enjoyed and were moved by (5). I leave it to you to guess whether they became involved, stayed together, and experienced changed lives.

VII. Programs and Activities. Strategic planning writers call this step "Tactics," which they define as the programs and activities that implement the strategy. Many churches want to begin here, skipping the first six steps in the process, in their haste to ride some "great new program," but a church only knows that a new program is great for them if it fits within their mission, builds upon a strength, engages an opportunity, serves an objective, and so forth. Generally, local churches rely far too much on imported prepackaged programs and resources, and far too little on their own entrepreneurial insights and innovativeness. Even worse, they passively wait for programs that do not yet exist and may never exist, as is exemplified by the pastor who said "no one has ever produced the right evangelism program for local churches like ours, and we are waiting until they do!"

Generally, the best-shaped programs and ministries are homegrown. The next best are adapted imported ideas and programs. The least effective are prepackaged programs imported blindly. Even so, there are just enough exceptions to these generalizations to keep us all on our toes.

Shepherd of the Valley Lutheran Church has become a credible example of innovative programming, built upon such variables as the strengths and emphasis of the pastor, the culture and needs of the people, and tight operational management. The objectives for persons—Get Right, Grow Right, Go right, and Glow Right—are featured in classes that meet for six weeks, four "semesters" a year. People take the Get Right class first, then the Grow Right class, and so on until they have completed all four. Each class is offered all four semesters, so there is always a new group of people entering the program. The Get Right class immerses people in the doctrine and reality of justification by grace through faith. The Grow Right class uses the Augsburg Catechism as its text. The Go Right class introduces people to the evangelistic ministry of the church and principles of Church Growth, using Win and Charles Arn's *Master's Plan for Making Disciples* as the text. The Glow Right course orients people to some of the classical disciplines and exercises of spiritual formation. People are received into the membership of the church after they have completed the Get Right seminar. They are received into the lay ministry of the church, joining "the priesthood of all believers," after completing the Glow Right seminar.

In each semester, many other classes are offered for the continuing formation of people. One popular seminar is held each semester for engaged couples; the course helps them to become friends! Another seminar focuses on people's gifts for ministry. The church's mission involves the deployment of hundreds of trained laypeople in ministries. People are then channeled into ministries for which they know themselves to be gifted by the Spirit, but regardless of each person's particular gift and ministry, all the people are continually coached in three concerns: for ministry, members, and multiplying.

The orchestration of all this is impressive. These Phoenix Lutherans secure and cultivate persons as prospects from a wide range of contacts—such as worship service registration pads, referrals from people in the community, names at baptismal classes, visitors of classes, engaged couples, weddings, funerals, and so forth. Each Sunday, the pastor stands out front before the service, identifying and greeting newcomers, and during the service he publicly recognizes members who have brought visitors. Again, a cadre of laypeople visit the hospitals. One woman, each Saturday night, calls the families of the hospitalized for support and updated reports; she reports to Hamlin at 10:00 P.M. He then focuses on the community concerns and pastoral prayer for the worship services the next morning.

VIII. Operational Plans. This is the second phase of the planning process, answering for each program and activity, Who will do what by when? Here, churches that have planned their work now move to work their plan. And, praise all that is Holy, most churches already know how to do it, and reasonably well. Even here some churches are making advances. The "PERT chart" method of scheduling and monitoring the progress of projects and keeping them on course is now fairly widely seen in churches, and some churches are now using computerized approaches to the operational management of their life and ministries.

Of course, the daily operations of some churches are badly managed. Their record keeping is episodic, the pastor's management of time is undisciplined, the budget is out of control, and some people with responsibilities do not know who will do what by when. In such churches, the detailed operational planning and management must be tackled and improved first. Consider such a church as needing "intensive care" for now. In a hospital's intensive care unit, you do not counsel a hemorrhaging patient about long-term life plans;

you first stop the hemorrhage. Some churches are intensive care churches. They need to get this week together before they are ready to consider the next decade.

Questions
About Strategic Planning for Churches

In field workshops and seminars, participants ask a lot of questions about strategic planning. Included here are three questions frequently asked, rather forcefully stated, and my responses—either given when the question arose or thought of later.

Q: Isn't strategic planning too "rational" a model? Life just isn't that tidy, predictable, and rational—particularly in organizations, especially in churches!

A: That's right. As G. K. Chesterton reminds us in *Orthodoxy*, "The problem with life is not that it is irrational. Nor is the problem with life that it is rational. The problem with life is that it is almost rational, that it appears slightly more rational than it is, and behind the appearance the wildness lies in wait!" In church organizational life, the wildness does erupt. Surprises sidetrack us. But with a strategic plan in place you may see the wildness sooner for what it is, you can cope with it through the mission and its objectives, and when the crisis is over you will not be immobilized—you will have the mission to return to.

Q: Why do all this planning? We value spontaneity, being able to move with the Spirit. Doesn't planning prevent inspiration?

A: The Holy Spirit can inspire us while we are planning as much as in the midst of action. In any case, the rationale of planning is not intended to prevent inspiration but to serve it. The most organized achievers "wing it" on occasion, but having a plan helps one distinguish between spontaneous inspiration and impulsive foolishness. As a parallel case, who is more likely to move with inspiration effectively, a preacher

207

who is prepared, or one who is not and will be winging it the whole twenty-five minutes?

Q: In the situation analysis, why do projections about the future? No one can predict the future!

A: Right again—though some future contingencies are much more likely than others. By the year 1995, it is possible that American car manufacturers could all go under and we would be buying cars made in Bolivia, but I'm not planning on it. So we state our best-informed assumptions about the future, knowing that "the only thing we know for sure about the future is that it will surprise us." We do not project a future scenario and make plans because we can predict the future, but because we cannot. In strategic planning, we state our best assumptions about what our world will be like in ten years and then plan on that basis. As the future unfolds *differently* from what we had expected, we know to *change* our plans accordingly.

In South Florida, a new congregation was started in the 1950s. The original leaders constructed a long-range plan, primarily a sequence of buildings to be built. When the last unit, a gymnasium, was constructed, the long-range plan would be fulfilled. The church grew more slowly than projected, but they built each building as they could afford it. Finally, some twenty-two years after the long-range plan's first step, they completed the original plan with the construction and dedication of the gym "to the glory of God." But the community around the church had changed in those twenty-two years, and by the time they started work on the gym, its original target population of unchurched teenagers was noticeably absent from the ministry area—if anyone was noticing. Today the gym stands, largely empty, as a memorial to a 1950s planning committee who penned some great ideas, but who neglected to state the assumptions about the future upon which they based their plans, and who neglected to say to successors: By the way, if the church's environment and opportunities develop differently from what we assumed they would in 1954, *do* modify the plans accordingly.

We state our assumptions about the future not because we can predict the future but because we cannot, and because some contingencies are more probable than others. We plan now with regard to our assumptions about the future, knowing that even the best laid plans may have to be altered as the real future unfolds. Leaders of historic Christian movements have adhered to this strategic flexibility in pursuing their objectives. Franz Hildebrandt (1956, p. 50) cites one of Wesley's lieutenants as saying: "Our Old Plan has been to follow the openings of Providence, and to alter and amend the plan, as we saw needful, in order to be more useful in the hand of God."

The Limits
of Church Growth

This book has shown something of the depth, range, and strategic importance of Church Growth literature to anyone who yearns to "spread the power of Jesus' name." Occasionally, overworked Christian leaders react to Church Growth theory with anxiety attacks over "*more* to do!" That feeling is understandable. But, once mastered, Church Growth knowledge liberates the time and energies of Christian leaders. They now work smarter and not necessarily harder. They now love the Lord of the Harvest with their minds as well as their hearts. Anxiety is now replaced by apostolic confidence. With clearer priorities and a vision of the way forward, their efforts are more productive and they become the achievers in apostolic ministry they were called to be. One pastor writes: "For years, I was a mere chaplain to people already Christians, now I'm a leader of the Christian movement in our city." Thus, enlightened Church Growth thought contributes much to the contagion of the Christian movement.

But strategic thought, even at its best, has its limits. It is fitting to conclude by acknowledging those limits and by suggesting the way to transcend them. The spread of Christianity is like a bonfire. Anyone who has ever built a bonfire knows how important is the placement of the kindling. You have no bonfire without effectively organizing the resources for burning. John Wesley knew much about effectively organizing the human resources for a Christian movement that spread like a well-planned bonfire, and from Church Growth we can now know more about organizing the sticks and logs than we have ever known before. Yet, as Alan Walker reminded the 1986 World Methodist Conference, "There is no campfire without fire. The Church today too often gives the impression of showing well-laid sticks without the fire." That fire is supplied only by the Holy Spirit. He gives the power for the spread of the gospel.

We do not organize or engineer the work of the Holy Spirit. Martin Luther spoke of the Holy Spirit as a wandering cloud—laden with moisture and wandering across the heavens, and no one knows when or where it will next drop down with its life-giving rain. But the Holy Spirit is not quite as unpredictable as Luther's analogy suggests. The rain is most likely to fall in a "low-pressure area," that is, where there is the least resistance. Indeed, where the people of God are most receptive, seeking that power with all their hearts, we are assured that the power will come in God's good time.

B I B L I O G R A P H Y

Abraham, William J. *The Coming Great Revival: Recovering the Full Evangelical Tradition.* San Francisco: Harper and Row, Publishers, 1984.

Ackoff, Russell L. *Redesigning the Future: A Systems Approach to Societal Problems.* New York: John Wiley and Sons, 1974.

Anderson, Andy, with Eugene Skelton. *Where Action Is.* Nashville: Broadman Press, 1976.

Anderson, E. S. *The Sunday School Growth Spiral.* Nashville: Sunday School Board of the Southern Baptist Convention, 1978.

Anderson, James D., and Ezra Earl Jones. *The Management of Ministry.* New York: Harper and Row, Publishers, 1978.

Arensberg, Conrad M., and Arthur H. Niehoff. *Introducing Social Change: A Manual for Community Development,* 2nd ed. New York: Aldine Publishing Co., 1971.

Aristotle, *The Rhetoric of Aristotle.* Trans. Lane Cooper. New York: Appleton-Century-Crofts, 1932.

Armstrong, Richard Stoll. *Service Evangelism.* Philadelphia: Westminster Press, 1979.

Arn, Win, and Charles Arn. *The Master's Plan for Making Disciples.* Pasadena, Cal.: Church Growth Press, 1982.

Asbury, Francis. *The Journal and Letters of Francis Asbury,* vols. 1-3. Nashville: Abingdon Press, 1958.

Ayling, Stanley. *John Wesley.* Cleveland: William Collins Publishers, 1979 (Abingdon edition, 1981).

Baker, Frank. *From Wesley to Asbury: Studies in Early American Methodism.* Durham, N.C.: Duke University Press, 1976.

Bartell, Floyd G. *A New Look at Church Growth.* Newton, Kan.: Faith and Life Press, 1979.

Baumann, Dan. *All Originality Makes a Dull Church.* Santa Ana, Cal.: Vision House Publishers, 1976.

Belew, M. Wendell. *Churches and How They Grow.* Nashville: Broadman Press, 1971.

Benjamin, Paul. *The Growing Congregation.* Lincoln, Ill.: Lincoln Christian College Press, 1972.

Bibliography

Burke, W. Warner. *Organization Development: Principles and Practices.* Boston: Little, Brown and Co., 1982.

Chaney, Charles L., and Ron S. Lewis. *Design for Church Growth.* Nashville: Broadman Press, 1977.
Chesterton, G. K. *Orthodoxy.* New York: Doubleday and Co., 1949.
Cho, Paul Y. *More Than Numbers.* Waco, Tex.: Word, 1984.
Conn, Harvey M., ed. *Theological Perspectives on Church Growth.* U.S.A.: Den Dulk Foundation, 1976.
Currie, Robert, Alan Gilbert, and Lee Horsley. *Churches and Churchgoers: Patterns of Church Growth in the British Isles Since 1700.* Oxford: Clarendon Press, 1977.

Davies, Rupert E. *Methodism.* Harmondsworth, Middlesex, England: Penguin Books, 1963.
Deal, Terrence E., and Allan A. Kennedy. *Corporate Cultures: The Rights and Rituals of Corporate Life.* Reading, Mass.: Addison-Wesley Publishing Co., 1982.
Donovan, Vincent J. *Christianity Rediscovered.* Chicago: Orbis Books, 1978.
Douglas, J. D., ed. *Let the Earth Hear His Voice.* Minneapolis, Minn.: World Wide Publications, 1975.
Douglass, Merrill E., and Donna N. Douglass. *Manage Your Time, Manage Your Work, Manage Yourself.* New York: Amacom, 1980.
Drucker, Peter F. *Management: Tasks, Responsibilities, Practices.* New York: Harper and Row, Publishers, 1973.
DuBose, Francis M. *How Churches Grow in an Urban World.* Nashville: Broadman Press, 1978.
Dudley, Carl S. *Making the Small Church Effective.* Nashville: Abingdon, 1978.
———. *Where Have All Our People Gone?* New York: Pilgrim Press, 1979.

Egan, Gerard. *The Skilled Helper,* 3rd ed. Monterey, Cal.: Brooks/Cole Publishing Co., 1986.
Engel, James F. *How Can I Get Them to Listen?* Grand Rapids: Zondervan Corp., 1977.
Engel, James F., and H. Wilbert Norton. *What's Gone Wrong with the Harvest?* Grand Rapids: Zondervan Corp., 1975.
Ensley, Francis Gerald. *John Wesley: Evangelist.* Nashville: Tidings, 1958.

Faulk, Peter. *The Growth of the Church in Africa.* Grand Rapids: Zondervan Corp., 1979.

Gopffarth, William. "TEE Today in the Philippines," from *Asia Theological News,* vol. 11, no. 3, 1985.

Harper, Steve. *John Wesley's Message for Today.* Grand Rapids: Zondervan Corp., 1983.
Hayford, Jack W. *The Church on the Way.* Grand Rapids: Zondervan Corp., 1983.
Hersey, Paul, and Ken Blanchard. *Management of Organizational Behavior: Utilizing Human Resources,* 4th ed. Englewood Cliffs, N.J.: Prentice-Hall, 1982.

Bibliography

Heitzenrater, Richard P. *The Elusive Mr. Wesley: Volume I.* Nashville: Abingdon Press, 1984.

——. *The Elusive Mr. Wesley: Volume II.* Nashville: Abingdon Press, 1984.

Hildebrandt, Franz. *Christianity According to the Wesleys.* London: Epworth Press, 1956.

Hoge, Dean R., and David A. Roozen, eds. *Understanding Church Growth and Decline: 1950–1978.* New York: Pilgrim Press, 1979.

Hogue, C. B. *I Want My Church to Grow.* Nashville: Broadman Press, 1977.

Hunter, George G., III. *. . . And Every Tongue Confess!: Toward a Recovery of Our Essential Mission.* Nashville: Discipleship Resources, 1983.

——. *The Contagious Congregation: Frontiers in Evangelism and Church Growth.* Nashville: Abingdon, 1979.

——. *Finding the Way Forward.* Nashville: Discipleship Resources, 1980.

Hunter, Kent R. *Foundations for Church Growth.* New Haven, Mo.: Leader Publishing Co., 1983.

Jackson, Thomas, ed. *The Works of John Wesley,* 3rd ed., vols. 1-14. Grand Rapids: Baker Book House, 1872 ed., reprinted 1978.

Jones, E. Stanley. *Conversion.* Nashville: Abingdon Press, 1959.

Jones, Ezra Earl. *Strategies for New Churches.* New York: Harper and Row, Publishers, 1976.

Keller, George. *Academic Strategy: The Management Revolution in American Higher Education.* Baltimore: Johns Hopkins University Press, 1983.

Kinghorn, Kenneth Cain. *Christ Can Make You Fully Human.* Nashville: Abingdon, 1979.

Kotler, Philip. *Marketing for Nonprofit Organizations,* 2nd ed. Englewood Cliffs, N.J.: Prentice-Hall, 1982.

Kraus, C. Norman, ed. *Missions, Evangelism, and Church Growth.* Scottdale, Pa.: Herald Press, 1980.

Kromminga, Carl C. *Bringing God's News to Neighbors.* Nutley, N.J.: Presbyterian and Reformed Publishing Co., 1975.

Lawson, E. Leroy, and Tetsunao Yamamori. *Church Growth: Everybody's Business.* Cincinnati: Standard Publishing, n.d.

Lee, Umphrey. *The Lord's Horseman: John Wesley the Man.* Nashville: Abingdon Press, 1954.

Luccock, Halford E. *Endless Lines of Splendor,* rev. ed. Evanston, Ill.: Commission on Promotion and Cultivation of the Methodist Church, 1964.

McGinnis, Alan Loy. *The Friendship Factor.* Minneapolis, Minn.: Augsburg Publishing House, 1979.

McGavran, Donald A., ed. *Church Growth and Christian Mission.* South Pasadena, Cal.: William Carey Library, 1965, 1976 reprint.

McGavran, Donald A. *The Bridges of God.* New York: Friendship Press, 1955.

——. *Church Growth in Mexico.* Grand Rapids: Wm. B. Eerdmans Publishing Co., 1963.

——. *Ethnic Realities and the Church.* Pasadena, Cal.: William Carey Library, 1979.

——. *Understanding Church Growth,* rev. ed. Grand Rapids: Wm. B. Eerdmans Publishing Co., 1980.

Bibliography

McGavran, Donald A. , and George G. Hunter III. *Church Growth: Strategies That Work*. Nashville: Abingdon, 1980.

McGavran, Donald A., and Win Arn. *How to Grow a Church*. Glendale, Cal.: G. L. Publications, 1973.

————. *Ten Steps for Church Growth*. New York: Harper and Row, Publishers, 1977.

McIntosh, Duncan, and Richard E. Rusbuldt. *Planning Growth in Your Church*. Valley Forge, Pa.: Judson Press, 1983.

McPhee, Arthur G. *Friendship Evangelism*. Grand Rapids: Zondervan Corp., 1978.

Miles, Delos. *Church Growth—A Mighty River*. Nashville: Broadman Press, 1981.

Miller, Herb. *Fishing on the Asphalt: Effective Evangelism in Mainline Denominations*. St. Louis: Bethany Press, 1983.

Montgomery, James H., and Donald A. McGavran. *The Discipling of a Nation*. Santa Clara, Cal.: Global Church Growth Bulletin, 1980.

Morris, George E. *The Mystery and Meaning of Christian Conversion*. Nashville: Discipleship Resources, 1981.

Murray, Dick. *Strengthening the Adult Sunday School Class*. Nashville: Abingdon, 1981.

Myers, Richard. *Program Expansion: the Key to Church Growth*. Privately published, n.d.

Mylander, Charles. *Secrets for Growing Churches*. New York: Harper and Row, Publishers, 1979.

Nida, Eugene A. "Culture and Church Growth," ch. 6 in *Church Growth and Christian Mission*, ed. Donald A. McGavran. Pasadena, Cal.: William Carey Library, 1976.

————. *Customs and Cultures*. South Pasadena, Cal.: William Carey Library, 1954.

————. "Dynamics of Church Growth," ch. 10 in *Church Growth and Christian Mission*, ed. Donald A. McGavran. Pasadena, Cal.: William Carey Library, 1976.

————. *Understanding Latin Americans*. South Pasadena, Cal.: William Carey Library, 1974.

Orjala, Paul R. *Get Ready to Grow*. Kansas City, Mo.: Beacon Hill Press, 1978.

Outler, Albert C. *Evangelism in the Wesleyan Spirit*. Nashville: Tidings, 1971.

————. *Theology in the Wesleyan Spirit*. Nashville: Tidings, 1975.

Parker, Percy Livingstone, ed. *The Journal of John Wesley*. Chicago: Moody Press, n.d.

Parvin, Earl. *Missions U.S.A*. Chicago: Moody Press, 1985.

Peters, Tom, and Nancy Austin. *A Passion for Excellence: The Leadership Difference*. New York: Random House, 1985.

Peters, Thomas J., and Robert H. Waterman, Jr. *In Search of Excellence: Lessons from America's Best-Run Companies*. New York: Harper and Row, Publishers, 1982.

Pickett, J. Wascom. *Christian Mass Movements in India*. Lucknow, India: Lucknow Publishing House, 1933.

————. *The Dynamics of Church Growth*. Nashville: Abingdon Press, 1963.

Rattenbury, J. Ernest. *Evangelism and Pagan England*. London: Epworth Press, 1954.

Bibliography

————. *Wesley's Legacy to the World.* London: Epworth Press, 1928.

Rogers, Everett M. *Diffusion of Innovations,* 3rd ed. New York: Free Press, 1983.

Schaller, Lyle E. *Activating the Passive Church: Diagnosis and ,Treatment.* Nashville: Abingdon, 1981.

————. *Assimilating New Members.* Nashville: Abingdon, 1978.

————. *The Change Agent.* Nashville: Abingdon Press, 1972.

————. *Effective Church Planning.* Nashville: Abingdon, 1979.

————. *Growing Plans.* Nashville: Abingdon Press, 1983.

————. *Hey, That's Our Church!* Nashville: Abingdon Press, 1975.

————. *The Middle-Sized Church: Problems and Prescriptions.* Nashville: Abingdon Press, 1985.

————. *The Multiple Staff and the Larger Church.* Nashville: Abingdon, 1980.

————. *Survival Tactics in the Parish.* Nashville: Abingdon, 1977.

Schmidt, Martin. *John Wesley: A Theological Biography,* vol. 1. Nashville: Abingdon Press, 1962.

————. *John Wesley: A Theological Biography,* vol. 2, part 1. Nashville: Abingdon Press, 1966.

————. *John Wesley: A Theological Biography,* vol. 2, part 2. Nashville: Abingdon Press, 1966.

————. *The Young Wesley: Missionary and Theologian of Missions.* London: Epworth Press, 1958.

Schuller, Robert H. *Your Church Has Real Possibilities!* Glendale, Cal.: G. L. Publications, 1974.

Seamands, John T. "The Role of the Holy Spirit in Church Growth," in *God, Man, and Church Growth,* ed. A. R. Tippett. Grand Rapids: Wm. B. Eerdmans Publishing Co., 1973.

————. *Tell It Well: Communicating the Gospel Across Cultures.* Kansas City, Mo.: Beacon Hill Press, 1981.

Shannon, Foster H. *The Growth Crisis in the American Church: A Presbyterian Case Study.* South Pasadena, Cal.: William Carey Library, 1977.

Shearer, Roy E. "The Psychology of Receptivity and Church Growth," in *God, Man, and Church Growth,* ed. A. R. Tippett. Grand Rapids: Wm. B. Eerdmans Publishing Co., 1973.

Smith, W. Douglas, Jr. *Toward a Continuous Mission: Strategizing for the Evangelization of Bolivia.* South Pasadena, Cal.: William Carey Library, 1978.

Snyder, Howard A. *The Radical Wesley and Patterns for Church Renewal.* Downers Grove, Ill.: InterVarsity Press, 1980.

Soper, Donald O. *The Advocacy of the Gospel.* Nashville: Abingdon Press, 1961.

————. *Popular Fallacies About the Christian Faith.* London: Epworth Press, 1938.

Steiner, George A. *Strategic Planning: What Every Manager Must Know.* New York: Free Press, 1979.

Stowe, David M. *Ecumenicity and Evangelism.* Grand Rapids: Wm. B. Eerdmans Publishing Co., 1970.

Sunda, James. *Church Growth in West New Guinea.* Lucknow, India: Lucknow Publishing House, 1963.

Tippett, Alan R. *Solomon Islands Christianity: A Study in Growth and Obstruction.* Pasadena, Cal.: William Carey Library, 1967.

Bibliography

Tregoe, Benjamin B., and John W. Zimmerman. *Top Management Strategy: What It Is and How to Make It Work.* New York: Simon and Schuster, 1980.
Tuttle, Robert G., Jr. *John Wesley: His Life and Theology.* Grand Rapids: Zondervan Corp., 1978.

Udy, Gloster S. *Key to Change.* Sydney, Australia: Donald F. Pettigrew Pty., 1962.

Wagner, C. Peter. *Leading Your Church to Growth.* Ventura, Cal.: Regal Books, 1984.
————. *Our Kind of People: The Ethical Dimension of Church Growth in America.* Atlanta, Ga.: John Knox Press, 1979a.
————. *Your Church Can Be Healthy.* Nashville: Abingdon, 1979b.
————. *Your Church Can Grow,* rev. ed. Ventura, Cal.: G. L. Publications, 1976.
Walrath, Douglas A. *Planning for Your Church.* Philadelphia: Westminster Press, 1984.
Watson, David Lowes. *Accountable Discipleship.* Nashville: Discipleship Resources, 1984.
Werning, Waldo J. *Vision and Strategy for Church Growth.* Chicago: Moody Press, 1977.
Williamson, Wayne B. *Growth and Decline in the Episcopal Church.* Pasadena, Cal.: William Carey Library, 1979.
Wood, A. Skevington. *The Burning Heart: John Wesley, Evangelist.* Minneapolis, Minn.: Bethany Fellowship, 1967.

Yamamori, Tetsunao, and E. Leroy Lawson. *Introducing Church Growth.* Cincinnati: Standard Publishing, 1975.

INDEX

Index

Index

Index